Crack___g
The Teen Code

How to find calm in the chaos

BRIAN COSTELLO

RIVERCLYDE
BOOKS

Published by Riverclyde Books
An imprint of Saltire Books Ltd
20 Main Street, Busby, Glasgow G76 8DU, Scotland
admin@rcbks.com

First published 2018

Typeset in the UK by Type Study, Scarborough in 10/13pt Novarese
Printed and bound in the UK by TJ International Ltd, Padstow

ISBN 978–1–908127–21–1 Print Edition
ISBN 978–1–908127–19–8 Digital Edition (mobi)
ISBN 978–1–908127–20–4 Digital Edition (epub)

The publisher makes no representation, express or implied, with regard to the accuracy of the information contained in this book and cannot accept any legal responsibility or liability for any errors or omissions that may be made.

The right of Brian Costello to be identified as the author of this work has been asserted in accordance with the UK Copyright, Designs and Patent Act 1988.

A catalogue record for this book is available from the British library.

Buzz Lightyear is a registered trademark of Disney Enterprises Inc.

Project management: Lee Kayne
Editorial: Katy McColl and Steven Kayne
Illustrations: Matt Canning
Cover design: Phil Barker

Contents

Foreword   **vii**

Preface   **xi**

Acknowledgements   **xv**

CHAPTER 1   The Curse of Parenthood   1

Adjusting to the demands of being a parent is a massive challenge. Back when it all began, your teenager was a blank canvas. Now they are on a mission to answer two big questions and this is only the beginning!

The Stages of Childhood   **7**

CHAPTER 2   Strictly Come Family   19

Every family uses a complex series of dances to remain stuck in a 'normal' that doesn't work. Understanding the reasons why you dance and how to break these unhelpful patterns of behaviour will begin the process of change. It's easier than you think, though it feels a bit weird at first!

Patterns   **27**

Pleasure and Pain   **43**

CHAPTER 3   To Infinity and Beyond   63

All their life, your teenager has been programmed by you but now their mind is taking them in new directions in a bid to answer their two big questions. Mistakes are inevitable and surprisingly, it's a cartoon character who teaches us that acceptance and understanding are the keys to change.

The Two Teen Questions   **75**

The Magic of Mistakes   **91**

CHAPTER 4   Yeah, No, Definitely, Maybe   107

Learning how to make good decisions is a big part of the teenage years but they struggle because they don't yet have the tools they need. You can help them if you understand what is going on and learn to spot the intention in their actions.

Mechanics of Mind: Experience   **111**
Mechanics of Mind: Models   **117**
Mechanics of Mind: Dilemma   **121**
Anxiety: The 'What If?' Problem   **127**
The Stages of Change   **141**

CHAPTER 5   Unstoppable Forces   153

Understanding the 'hows' and, more importantly, the 'whys' of motivating your teenager is an essential skill for parents. We also take a look at codes, rules, missions and the importance of being like toilet paper!

The Levels of 'Why?' – Levels 1 & 2   **159**
The Rules for Rules   **169**
The Levels of 'Why?' – Levels 3 & 4   **175**

CHAPTER 6   Too Much, Too Young   191

Your teenager is under enormous pressure from the modern world and their emotional states are leaking all over your house! Many of their issues are actually illusions that you can learn to break with a few simple questions. Really? Yes, really.

Spotting Stress   **197**
Dealing with Depression   **207**

CHAPTER 7   Being Good People   231

And finally, we put it all together and learn the six most powerful words in the universe.

Epilogue: Being Number One   **239**
An Ending Introduction   **251**

For J *and* A

My *motivation and inspiration*

Foreword

Hello, my name is Jodie and I'm a teenager.

I've actually been a teenager for a few years now, since 11th March 2012 to be precise when, contrary to my expectations, my mindset did not abruptly change from 'child' on 10th March to 'teen' the next day.

Every year we ask each other, "do you feel any older?" and every year, a part of us expects to, or at least feel different in some way. On 11th March 2012 I expected there to be a sudden cataclysmic change in my core DNA that would affect the very essence of my being and change who I was as a person.

But that didn't happen. Nothing really did, other than a lovely meal with my family and a balloon or two.

I was just a year older.

Five years later, 11th March 2017 marked my 18th birthday. Despite my previous experience, once again contrary to my expectations, my mindset did *not* abruptly change from 'teen' on 10th March to 'adult' the next day.

Nothing really changed this time either. Other than another lovely family meal, I was just a year older.

There's no doubt that my life goals, values, knowledge and experience changed during my teenage years, as has my personality. But

I can't tell you *when* these things started to change. It might have been when I was 13, 15, 17, or somewhere else in the timeline. I can't even tell you exactly *what* changed or *how* – you'd have to ask my parents and sister about that – but I look back now on 13 year old Jodie with slightly fuzzy recollections. At her core, she might have been exactly the same person as I am now, or she might have been completely different. I don't truly know because I don't remember much. I can't even tell you what colour her hair was!

Aside from the family holidays and other events documented in photo albums, the things I *do* remember from age 13 are school and my parents. The philosopher Alan Watts once said "when you send a child to school, your child is brought up by all the other children"[1] and I think this is entirely accurate, possibly going a long way to explaining why parents seem to think that all teenagers in a group act vaguely similar. I definitely learned a lot from my peers; *most* of it good, but some lessons I may have been able to live without.

While writing this foreword, I began to think back to what my parents were like five years ago and, at first, I was slightly concerned that I couldn't remember them being any different to the way they are today. But soon I began to understand that the personalities and core values of parents, like the majority of older people, are relatively static compared to the ever-changing, kaleidoscopic world of a teenager. So the fact that I can say with some certainty that, in many respects, my parents are the same people now that they were five years ago, is actually immensely comforting. I know the kind of people they were then and they are the same people now.

I'm only now beginning to understand how it must feel to them when they can't say the same about me.

---

[1] Lecture titled Education for Non-Entity (available at www.alanwatts.com).

This book will show you that being a teenager is not a disease – it is simply a phase of life. It can be a crazy, difficult, confusing, upsetting and weird phase of life, but that's all it is. I don't remember a lot of the stuff that happened in the last five years and that doesn't matter because, in the grand scheme of life, I'm fairly sure that one day I'll understand that the teenage years didn't matter much at all. But when you are living them, whether as a teen or a parent, that fact is massively difficult to appreciate.

It's easy to make the teenager the villain when things go wrong in the family dynamic. Many parents do this but it's not always fair and never helps the situation. When reading this book you will begin to understand how simple acceptance and understanding of the issues troubling teens can bring great clarity to the situation. After all, these are the same issues that trouble all humans, just sprinkled with a lack of experience, underdeveloped decision making skills and a lot of extra hormones to make everything a little bit more fiery than it needs to be.

The American spiritual teacher Ram Dass famously said, 'in most of our human relationships, we spend much of our time reassuring each other that our costumes of identity are on straight.'[2] As a teenager, this costume is slowly being adapted and re-worked until even we don't fully recognise it any more. This book is a reminder to all who read it that teenagers are just humans who are still figuring out who they are and that's OK. It's up to you, as their parent, to help them.

For teenagers, this book is a reassuring voice when trying to figure out who you *are* rather than who you were programmed to be. It is there for you whilst you unpick the parts of your parents that were frantically stitched on to you to protect you from the outside

---

[2] The official Ram Dass website (www.ramdass.org – relationship quotes section).

world. It is there for you so you can understand how your parents struggle whilst raising someone that is going through so many overwhelming changes. It is there to remind you that the things you are going through are not just *you* things but *human* things.

For parents, this book will act as a helping hand for those times where you can't see yourself in your children any more. It can be a reminder that they are no longer babies looking up at you waiting to be told what to do and how to be. Now, they are looking around them to those who walk on the same level, who they believe understand them better than you do. In this book you'll learn that acting to stop mistakes before they happen is less effective than dealing with them appropriately when they do.

I've heard that parenting can be a dark and complicated place, especially when it comes to the teenage years and that can be terrifying. Just like being a teenager, I imagine it feels like you have taken a series of wrong turns to end up so lost in a place like this.

This book is the map we all need.

Now you can do what I have done throughout my life when I've been confused and not sure which direction to turn.

You can ask my dad for help.

He wrote the book you are now holding.

* * * *

Jodie Costello is in her first year at St. Andrews University, studying English Literature. She has won awards for creative writing, being short-listed for Warwick University's Iggy Litro prize in 2016.

Preface

Like most of you, when I was a teenager I just wanted to find someone that had the answers. And probably like most of you, I was still looking for them when I became an adult. In fact, it wasn't actually until after I became a parent that the answers finally began to appear.

***

In 2003, I experienced my first introduction to the world of psychology and personal development . . . and *everything* changed! It ignited a passion in me to study, read, learn and teach as much as I possibly could about the subject. This passion continues to this day and has always been driven by one very personal purpose – to use my knowledge to help young people.

In the early days of my passion, my own children were very young, only 2 and 4 years old. At that time, they were not the young people I was passionate about helping, at least not yet. Young children gain most of their emotional understanding from their parents. If you are generally a happy, positive and well balanced individual, your kids are likely to follow your lead. They adopt your personality traits and they will mimic your behaviour and your view of the world, to a certain age at least.

That doesn't mean we grow up without fears, anxieties or emotional moments. It's just that, in many cases throughout our early years, a cuddle from mum or dad can cure anything and a wise parental word can reset our emotions.

All that changes when we become teenagers.

You see, the young person I was most interested in helping first was *me*. More specifically, 16 year old me.

* * *

When I think back to my earliest memories of childhood, I remember spending most of my time generally mucking about with my friends. That was my life. School wasn't taken that seriously and was considered more of a temporary interruption to playing. Of course we learned things there but there was no real pressure to do well in exams or think about the future.

Another constant presence in my life that I didn't really think about was the idea of family and I just accepted it was there. I enjoyed spending time with all my family, both close and extended and staying over with my grandparents was a particular treat. I also enjoyed baking cakes, playing football, running about with my pals and computer games.

And then at about the age of 13, everything changed.

Life became more serious. School became more important – there were exams, reports and questions about my ability and application. Time for playing became less frequent with grown up conversations and activities in its place. My social life changed beyond recognition and that meant, especially in my later teens, family became less important to me. In fact, if I'm honest, it became more of an interruption to all the other things going on in my life and now, as I look back, it is with some regret.

By the time I was 16 I had left the safety of school and I was a little lost. I'd become a semi-adult but I had no idea who I was or what I was doing. I was really just coasting through life, a kind of emotional chameleon, being exactly who people wanted me to be rather than truly being myself.

This is the young person I wanted to help when I gained all my personal development knowledge.

And urgently . . . because I was still this lost soul when I became a parent.

***

I read a quote online recently that urged me to 'be the person you needed when you were younger' and I think that perfectly sums up the focus of this book.

When I was a teenager, I didn't know exactly who I needed but I do know that they weren't there.

It wasn't that my parents didn't help me, on the contrary, I wouldn't let them help as much as they wanted to. I pushed them away because in my mind, they didn't really understand what was going on or who I really was. They couldn't help me, no-one could. It was just easier, safer and more convenient to find solace and support with my friends.

The problem with being a teenager finding solace with your friends is that all your friends are going through exactly the same stuff and none of them know what is going on either! How can you get help from someone who is just as stuck as you are?

And we don't stop even when we become parents. We continue making it up as we go along and thinking it would be really useful if there was an instruction manual to make sense of what's going on.

This book is a collection of observations, thoughts and methods that I have studied, used and taught. The guidance in these pages has been tried and tested by the many parents and teenagers who have been my clients and those who have attended my seminars, workshops and courses.

I know you that up to now you have been doing your very best and, as you will read, it's OK to need help. I can't promise an instant improvement in your family dynamic, but if you adapt what you learn in these pages to your own circumstances and really want to make positive changes, things *will* get easier.

As a parent, I want this book to help you find your teenager and be the 'person they need'.

As a teenager, I want this book to help you see that your parents do understand and can help.

I want this book to help you all make sure no-one in your family stays lost.

Brian Costello
Glasgow, Scotland
December 2017

Acknowledgements

Writing a book like this is not a solo endeavor and for that reason there are a few very important people that require a public dedication of gratitude.

Firstly my daughters, Jodie and Amy, who have been my unwitting test subjects for their whole lives. I ask them to always remember that life, like science, requires as many failures as successes to advance.

To my wife, Sheena. Now, I'm not saying that any of the tips, tricks, techniques and wisdom in this book are really hers . . . but if they *were*, then I know she'd let me claim them as my own because she loves me unconditionally.

To my parents, Margaret and Terry and my grandparents, Nell and John. Each of you were a role model to me. I know that many of the things I do right, many of the things that have helped me be a good parent and even the fact that I've now written two books, are all because of your influence.

To my teachers, inspirations and motivators, I thank you all for your teaching, writings and guidance, especially Richard Bandler, John Grinder, Morris Massey, Tony Robbins, Byron Katie, Steve Burns, Owen Fitzpatrick and many others.

I am convinced, for many reasons, that this book would not be in existence if it wasn't for the tireless and expert work of my editor. Thank you Lee for making my words readable.

And to the wider publishing, editing and production team, Katy, Steven and their team of readers, your patience and kindness in dedicating your time to helping me figure out what is and isn't working is valued more than you'll ever know. On this book, I think Phil, Dave and Matt have surpassed even the last one with cover, page design and illustrations respectively – thanks so much for your amazing work once again.

I must thank all the parents who have entrusted me with their teenager's minds over the last 10 years. By contributing to the progression of my understanding, each of you have helped many more teenagers than just your own.

And finally, to all those teenagers themselves, who have sat in my client chair, answered my silly questions, played my silly games, given honest answers. We've laughed, we've cried and we've made interesting, revealing and sometimes difficult discoveries together. I thank you all for your trust.

This book exists both *for* you and *because* of you.

"When we bring children into the world we play awful games with them. Instead of saying, 'How do you do? Welcome to the human race. Now my dear, we are playing some very complicated games and these are the rules of the game we are playing. I want you to understand them and to learn them and then when you get a little bit older you might be able to think up some better rules.' Instead of being quite direct with our children, instead we say 'you're here on probation, you understand that? And maybe when you grow up a bit you'll be acceptable but until then you should be seen and not heard. You're a mess. And you've got to be educated and schooled and whipped until you are human.'"

Alan Watts (1915–1973) in a lecture titled *Myth of Myself* from the *Tao of Philosophy* series (www.alanwatts.com)

1
The Curse of Parenthood

Let's start out by making one thing clear. There is just one certainty you have as a parent, one guaranteed outcome of parenthood.

In my humble opinion, anyone attempting to become a parent and pass their genes on to the next generation should be warned about this well in advance, because, if we knew this fact from the moment our new creation popped into the world, parenting would be a whole lot easier. In fact, we'd probably stop stressing about it anywhere near as much as we do.

Here it is, the one, guaranteed outcome of parenthood . . .

something you do is going to mess your kid up.

It's not a matter of if, maybe, might or possibly. It's going to happen. It's just a matter of what and when. After you've done it, you won't even realise exactly what you've done until it's way too late and then, once you start the belated process of trying to correct your mistakes, your wee baby will be a teenager and everything will be total chaos.

Once they are a teenager, they will have far more exciting things to do than listen to you telling them over and over how you don't want them to 'make the same mistakes you made at this age'.

You're too late. It's done. You did it. And now there's *nothing* you can do to change it.

Well, almost nothing . . .

The first thing you can do to begin a process of change is to pick up this book, so congratulations on completing that important step! The next is to understand that in most cases, things are rarely as bad as they seem. Even when they seem really, really bad, they are still, not as bad as they seem. And the final one is to accept that changes on *all* sides are going to be needed to address the problems.

Your teenager may seem like they are some strange unknown alien species but really they are a unique kind of *human*. Yes, really they are. Just like you. Except that you have joined a strange, all-knowing subgroup of humans who dispense advice and guidance accumulated through a life time of experience gained by not following that advice and guidance. We call this subgroup 'parents' and they are just another unique kind of human. And they were even teenagers once.

The aim of this book is to help you think less like a parent and more like a human. At that point you'll understand more, stress less and maybe start to enjoy watching someone you love grow into a happy and fulfilled adult.

If that seems too scary right now, that's fine. Put the book down and retreat to a safe distance, then come back when the time is right. I'll be right here . . .

. . .

Ready to go? Let's begin . . .

THE BLISS OF IGNORANCE

First we need to understand how our minds are made and look at the psychology of why the hormonal bag of mood swings that masquerades as your son or daughter acts the way they do.

Let's go back to the beginning.

Remember the joy/fear/happiness/horror/accomplishment/surprise[1] that you felt when you found out your baby was on the way?

Remember keeping your pregnancy secret, at least for a while, hoping things will be OK but with a million 'What if . . .?' questions stopping you from getting properly excited? 'What if something goes wrong?', 'What if I don't eat properly?', 'What if we split up and I end up on my own?'

Chances are, you didn't even relax when the doctor looked at that first scan and told you, officially, that everything looked good, healthy and proper.

What a day that was. You went for that first scan and technology I don't even pretend to understand gave you the chance to see your little prince or princess for the first time in grainy, blurry monochrome. It was a special moment, a moment where all those initial feelings of fear and excitement flood over you (possibly joined by a few new ones too!) and you felt ready to start spreading the news. Remember how you enjoyed the faces as you told friends and family – pride, shock, joy, sympathy and my personal favourite the 'are you sure this is a good idea' face?

Can you remember the moment when you realised what you'd got yourself into? Remember when your whole world changed in front

---

[1] Delete as appropriate.

of your eyes? Shops that you swear never existed before appeared from nowhere, selling things you have no idea why you needed? You became proficient in discussions regarding multi point fixed car seats, the folding mechanisms of pushchairs and ergonomically designed anti-colic bottles, pretending you knew what you were talking about but actually making it up as you went along. You whizzed round Mothercare 'testing' transportation equipment with features such as 'free floating wheel design' like you had a damn clue what was going on. Then, if you're anything like me, you wondered whether it would be easier to just buy a new car than fight to get this bloody thing folded into the current family saloon.

You looked at racks of tiny little clothes and as the date drew near you couldn't help but wonder what your new arrival will be like. Will they have a style? What will their voice be like? What colour of hair will they have? Will they have your nose? What will you call them?

You read books and magazines packed with pictures of smiling people who make this whole parenting thing look like it will be a breeze of warm, summer mornings, soft skin cuddles, lavender scented nappies, organic vegetables, polite burping and joy. It was probably around this time that the panic started to set in, when you finally became aware that everything was about to change forever.[2]

I mean, before the birth there are anxieties and worries, but it's not until the big day that the real change starts. The moment the midwife or doctor puts the baby in your arms, you realise that you have just become a *parent*.

---

[2] As many of you will know, this is often considerably different for second and subsequent new humans, who have been known to reach the age of 3 before anyone really notices!

A mum.

A dad.

It is amazing and exhilarating and daunting and maybe even terrifying. That wee grainy image from your scan is now a real, living, breathing person.

And it's yours.

Even in the first few seconds of his or her arrival, this brand new human has already changed your life. And they continue to do so as you sit here reading these pages.

It often seems that everything that happened in those early years was just a blur, but actually childhood has three distinct stages. Understanding these stages is the key to learning what is going on as your child grows up.

The Stages of Childhood

Stage 1 – Learning what to do
Stage 2 – Learning what we like
Stage 3 – Learning who we are

Now, I know you are reading this book to learn about your teenager. However, by looking back at these earlier stages of life, you will start to see that the problems, issues and dramas you are dealing with today often have their roots way, way back in time.

Let's start at the beginning . . .

STAGE 1 – LEARNING WHAT TO DO

For about the first seven years of our existence we are all pretty much bouncing from one interesting thing to the next, simply wondering what the world actually is.

If you can remember back to your own early years, you'll remember that things were largely black and white. The answer to most questions was a straight 'yes' or 'no' which, while making life simple, is at the same time, hugely frustrating!

There's an old joke that asks, 'what's the difference between a crazed bank robber holding 10 hostages and a 2 year old?' The answer? 'You can reason with a bank robber!'

Psychologically, this stage is all about your child testing out the world;

What is good?
What is bad?
Is what I am doing 'right' or 'wrong'?

And by far the biggest little question . . .

Why?

Why is the sky up there?
Why are cats funny?
Why does poo smell?
Why can't I take my whole bucket of sand home from the beach?

These questions may seem pointless to grown ups but they are absolutely vital to your child's growth. You have given birth to an empty vessel with no knowledge of the world. You are the main teacher, you have the knowledge and you are the best person to ask. Of course you can only teach them *your* understanding of the world, but as far as they are concerned your understanding is 100% accurate. There is nothing else.

So what did you teach them?

Let's look at some examples of classic early teaching.

'Spiders are horrible, scary things'
Now, inside that young impressionable mind, because you've told them so, spiders are very likely to have become 'horrible, scary things'.

'People that <insert questionable behaviour here> are bad'
The little developing brain you've been put in charge of won't question this sort of wisdom and can easily end up perceiving that behaviour as bad for the rest of their lives. Did you really mean for that to happen? Is it as bad as you made it out?

'I love you so much'
This phrase means a huge amount to someone learning how the world works. Of course they will not fully understand the word 'love' so they will pay attention to whatever happens just before or just after you've said it. This is really important – to a young child the actions that precede and/or follow words are exactly what those words mean.

So did you teach,

Love = cuddles + playtime?

Or did you teach that love means something else?

And what other words did you teach them? Words like 'shy' or 'angry'? What does it mean when someone cries because they are upset? Does that mean they are weak? Does it mean they are silly? Or does it mean that they should come and find you so you can help?

Think about it.

Remember, this isn't about blaming yourself or anyone else. It's about understanding where things started so that we can do whatever we need to undo any mistakes we may have made.

STAGE 2 – LEARNING WHAT WE LIKE

Around the age of seven, parents start to notice a change in the way our children interact with the world. The soft, fluffy edges of early childhood begin to wear off and we become acutely aware that we are being watched and, much more importantly, we are being imitated.

Now the basic rules of life have been established, it is time for our growing humans to start their long journey to becoming a well-rounded member of society. But there is something vitally important that our kids have to do before they can take their place in society and become themselves – they have to try being everyone else first!

As a parent, this stage is punctuated with frequent comments from friends and family about 'How grown up they are' and 'I can't believe that's your wee baby' as your little girl starts showing little flashes of womanhood and your little boy starts showing the merest hints of adult masculinity.

But you have to remember, all those years ago, you gave birth to a blank canvas. There is only one way to work out how to become an individual member of society in their own right. They need to find a teacher and practice.

That teacher is you.

Imitating you is the practice.

The result can be annoyingly unpredictable!

Think back to your early years, age 8, 9 or 10, and think about all the things you saw and experienced that have influenced the person you are today.

When I was growing up, my Uncle Chris always seemed so exciting. He always had nice cars and one of my earliest memories of being with him is trying to convince him to buy a convertible in a Glasgow car showroom, unaware that the concepts of 'convertible' and 'Glasgow' were not ideally suited to each other, particularly in January! But, to little excitable me, the car had no roof on it and was just the coolest thing I had ever seen – Uncle Chris was cool so why *wouldn't* he want the coolest car in the showroom?

Despite rejecting my admittedly pretty flawed motoring choices, Uncle Chris always appeared to me to be a fun, happy, calm and all round awesome guy. As I marched towards my teenage years, I always looked up to him as the type of man I wanted to be when I grew up and inevitably, I began to be unconsciously influenced by his choices and 'tried them on' for myself.

For example, it was because he liked Queen and Dire Straits that I learned the joy of a Freddie Mercury performance and a Mark Knopfler guitar solo. My Uncle Chris saw Queen live at Wembley Stadium in 1986 and to a 13 year old looking for a hero, that was just the most amazing thing ever. What a life to live. I wanted that when I grew up. I didn't know what that really meant, how I would get there or even if it was a difficult thing to achieve. I just wanted to be like Uncle Chris.

This is how aspiration works. This is how young people shape their dreams.

Uncle Chris wasn't the only influence on my life of course, and I tried on different aspects of many people. Obviously my parents were a major influence, other relatives, friends, teachers, celebrities on the TV (which is the only place I can imagine that my very early career aspiration of professional tap dancing originated) and everyone around me.

And this isn't just something I did, we all did it. You will have aspects of your personality that have come from those around you as you grew up. Don't tell me you have never uttered the words 'Oh no, I am turning into my Mum/Dad!!'. I know you have. And that's simply because they were some of your most influential, powerful and most unconscious of teachers.

But now you are a parent and that means you have a real responsibility to be a good teacher.

You are the first other person your child will 'try on'.

Could it possibly be that your stubborn teen learned their stubbornness from watching and imitating you?

Or maybe it's not stubbornness at all and they simply listened closely to your advice to 'never give up if you think that you're right'. Maybe the real issue is they currently lack the skills required to apply the things they have learned in the proper context.

For example, 'never give up if you think that you're right' might be great advice for life in general, but when they believe they are 100% right about staying out to 3am and not letting you know where they are, you may need to tweak your teaching!

Or what if your child is showing anxiety or is uncomfortable in social situations? How did they learn to be that way? When they were young, did they unwittingly pay attention to your anxiety and awkwardness in social settings and have now taken that on for themselves as an effective way to keep themselves safe?

Or perhaps they tried on your casual, outgoing, friendly nature only to find it wasn't reciprocated by friends at school. In the absence of another teacher to show them another way to be, they now avoid social interaction at all costs?

Up to about age 14, your teenager is 60–70% a mirror of you, with the remainder being the other significant people they spend time with. If you look carefully, and you are honest with yourself, you'll see yourself, right there looking back at you.

But they're not finished. Oh no, they've still got one hefty stage of emotional growth in front of them and, for you as parent, the real work is only just about to begin.

Now we get to the real reason we are here.

It's teen time!

STAGE 3 – LEARNING WHO WE ARE

Think lion!

Have you ever watched one of those wildlife programmes where a now adolescent Simba, who we have watched grow and develop from a wee, cute fluffy lion cub, is forced out of the pride to go off and fend for himself? A concerned commentator adopts a serious tone and dramatic minor chords play as Simba tries to convince his mum to let him stay. Eventually daddy lion comes along and shows him there is no place for him in this pride any more and we watch as the inexperienced youngster wanders off into the expanse of jungle or savannah.

Alone.

Lion parents know that their little boy must go off and find a life for himself and, being responsible parents, will do whatever it takes to get him to leave and discover what life is really about.

It's part of the growing process.

Lions are good at this. Humans are not.

Your teenager will stop imitating you at around 14 years old. However, it's important to remember that, because of the way learning works, we never truly stop 'trying on' other people – we will spend our whole lifetime adopting, adapting and grafting other people's skills and attributes to ourselves. We call this *modelling* and we'll talk more about it later.

However, as a full time developmental pursuit, age 14 is about the time that 'trying on' takes a back seat and a new period of chaos (a.k.a. personal discovery) begins! We'll look at this in more detail a little later on.

Your little baby, who popped into the world as a blank canvas all those years ago, who you have nurtured and cared for, who you have watched grow and become an awesome little human being is now ready to step out of your shadow and become 'themselves'.

But that requires them to find the answers to two crucially important questions, simple to ask but far more difficult to answer. We're going to call these the Two Teen Questions and we will refer to them repeatedly throughout the rest of this book.

The Two Teen Questions are:

Who Am I?

and

How Do I Fit in?

Before we go on, let me ask if you remember when and/or how *you* answered these questions?

Have you, even now as a fully grown human, found real, definitive answers?

If you have, are they answers that you are completely comfortable with?

If your answer is 'yes', I congratulate you! And I promise that you are in a very tiny minority!

Whatever your answer, you know from your personal experience that no-one can help you with these questions. You might have asked other people such as your parents and those people closest to you, and they may have helped a little but the answers can only *truly* be discovered by one person.

And that's the person asking them.

So for your teen, after 14 years of support, 14 years of care, 14 years of advice, 14 years of understanding, 14 years of following, their mind is suddenly forcing them out on their own.

Their mind is telling them it is time to leave the pride.

It's time to go it alone.

And that's a problem.

Because very often, they don't want to. And, as parents, we don't want them to either! We've had 14 years to get used to keeping them safe, warm, fed and clothed and to be quite honest, we like things the way they are. Why do they have to grow up?

Oh sure, we *say* we're prepared for them to go out on their own . . .

"Soon it'll be time for you to fly the nest and I'm going to walk round the house naked all the time."

"Your Dad and I can't wait for you to leave, we're going to spend all our savings on Caribbean holidays and drink gin for breakfast."

"It's time for you to look after me now. Get me the biscuits from the cupboard and put the kettle on, will you?"

In truth though, we are all afraid of change.

No-one wants things to change at such a young age. But they do. And, as hard as it is, you have to let them. You can't stop things changing and you can't cling on to the cute, ten year old, bright eyed beauty you remember from the photographs because that time is gone. Your wee baby has grown up and it is your parental responsibility to let them find their own answers.

Of course that doesn't mean you cast them out and refuse to engage with the process. Even as they proclaim 'I should just be allowed to be myself', now more than ever, their teenage mind needs guidance and support to navigate this tempestuous time of life. Their growing mind might not *want* your guidance and support, but that doesn't mean that it doesn't *need* it!

There is no way out. You're in this now. You can't run and you can't hide. Even if you tried, it would still happen anyway. Your role as a parent is more important now than it ever has been.

You are still their teacher, their guide, their mentor, leader, perhaps even their friend.

Your child is getting ready to leave the pride. It is nearly time for them to go off into the expanse of uncertainty we call adulthood and fend for themselves.

But they're not quite ready yet.

There is still much to learn . . . for everyone.

Chapter 1 – What The . . . ?

- Accept it; something you do is going to mess your kid up. It might have already happened and you've not even noticed. You didn't mean it, it's not your fault, everything is going to be OK.

- There are three stages of childhood:
  - Learning what to do
  - Learning what we like
  - Learning who we are

- Every human was born a blank canvas and through all their stages, the most important, and often first, teacher for your human was you.

- Now you own a teenager, watch for the Two Teen Questions:
  - Who Am I?
  - How Do I Fit In?

2
Strictly Come Family

If you had to guess, what would you think is the biggest problem that parents face when dealing with their teenagers?

Lack of communication?

Unpredictable mood swings?

No common ground?

What if it's much more basic that that? What if the biggest problem parents face when dealing with their teenagers is simply what they all consider to be 'normal'.

I call this concept of 'normality', the *'dance'*.

You may not immediately recognise yourself as someone with a natural talent for rhythm but, if you are part of a family or any group of people numbering more than one (I'm going to assume you are involved with at least one other human being!), I can guarantee, you are a skilled dancer.

You see, as you read on and begin to understand how people work, you will begin to see all of your family's arguments, emotional explosions, sulks, huffs, slammed doors, and begrudgingly cleaned rooms in a different way. You will begin to see that almost every moment in your family life is a small step in a suite of bigger, more complex and surprisingly elaborate 'dances'.

Without even noticing it, you have dedicated more hours of practice to these 'dances' than to most other things in your life. You have been unconsciously refining and perfecting your steps in them for at least 13 years and perhaps much, much longer.

So what *is* the biggest problem that parents face when dealing with their teenagers?

The biggest problem is that no one actually realises they are dancing.

TINY DANCERS

The amazing author, speaker and change worker Byron Katie once said "You can't change what you haven't realized yet. Once you realize what you were asleep to, the change happens on its own."[1]

What Katie is saying is, that you cannot change anything if you do not realise there is a problem. When a parent calls me to help their teenager, I always ask 'Do *they* know there is a problem?'. If they don't then I tend to advise the parent *against* bringing their teenager for help at this stage.

Ask yourself, if I appeared in your life right now and asked you to change something you didn't think was a problem, what would you say to me? Say I told you that you need to change your job because I think you are working too hard. Or stop seeing a close friend because I think they are toxic to your life. Or that you need to break up your relationship because I think your partner is unhealthy for you.

Would you just blindly agree with me and do what I say?

---

[1] The Work of Byron Katy. http://www.thework.com

I don't think you would. Why would you change if you don't believe there is a problem?

This is how our dances begin. Two opposite perspectives on the same issue. This is why, in my experience, many parents and teenagers become active partners in dances they are not even aware they are performing! It becomes normal. The argument, the angry word, the shouting, the tension, the avoidance, the sullen face, the problem that isn't talked about, whatever it is in your family. We become used to it and because both sides think they are right, neither side thinks it is a problem.

And, as we just said,

change won't happen until you accept the problem.

Let's look at a couple of the more popular and well loved dances, performed in families all over the world.

THE 'SAME OLD THING' WALTZ

This dance is first performed when children are about 6 or 7 years old, able to think for themselves and understand the basic rules of life that we discussed in Chapter 1. In the early months and years, while a family is still practicing this special routine, it is only occasionally performed. However, as the years pass, many families find this becomes an extensively practiced part of their daily dancing routine.

Often, when it is performed, it begins quietly, without fuss, almost unnoticed.

In a corner of the house, some important chore, activity or task, e.g. washing of dishes, cleaning of clothes, tidying of rooms, is simply *not* being done.

In that perfect moment of inactivity, the dance has begun

And now we wait . . .

Eventually one of the parental dancers will take lead when they notice the task has not been done. Bringing this fact to the attention of the family usually initiates an immediate, loud and/or abrasive response from one or more of the younger members of the troupe.

This new performer (the blamed) takes the floor to perform their part in the dance. Their moves may take the form of claiming a lack of knowledge of the task ("I didn't know I was meant to do it . . .") or they may choose a more advanced option, such as attempting to deflect blame to another dancer ("I wasn't asked to do it, you asked [sibling] to do it"). Especially common in larger groups, they may go straight for a direct finish ("it's [sibling]'s turn") and attempt to leave the dancefloor as quickly as they can. But this is not always possible and they may find themselves fully involved until the dance reaches its exciting crescendo.

The lead dancer (the parent), driven by teenage rebuttal, may make a sarcastic comment, hinting subtly or otherwise, that whatever happens or whoever's 'turn' it is, the task must still be done. A loop of indeterminate length has now begun and, as we enter the final phase, it is normal for the dance to become significantly more intense. The experience and skill of the dancers will now determine how quickly the dance concludes – it has been known for some families to run these loops for extended periods.

"It still needs to be done."

   "It's not my turn, it's his/hers."

"No it's not, it's yours."

   "But I did it last week."

"No that was the week before."

   "It was last week."

"Anyway, I don't care, it still needs to be done."

   "But it's not my turn, it's his/hers."

"No it's not . . ."

Dramatic movements and some shouting drive the dance onward as it builds towards the explosive finale, always performed by one of the parents with maximum exasperation . . .

"Why do I have to say the same *$#*^! thing, every single *$#*^! day?"

And with that, the dance enters its closing act, though it should be noted that it is just as likely that the dance will continue in a loop until the original task is completed.

By anyone.

Doesn't matter who.

Just someone do it please.

THE 'YOU HAVE NO IDEA WHAT IT'S LIKE' TWO STEP

This modern classic is driven by our teenage dancers and can often appear, to the uninitiated observer at least, to be an entirely solo dance. However, those skilled in family choreography will notice the subtle but vital part played by parents in a dance that often ends in emotional outbursts and rounds of percussive door slamming. In some extreme performances, it has been known for household ceramics to be broken or even shoes to be thrown.

The first steps of this dance are often taken outside the home with secretive rounds of teen-only dances such as the inimitable 'This Teacher Is Rubbish' tango, the dramatic and hopefully rare 'What Do You Mean Detention, It Wasn't Me' boogaloo or even a quick recital of the solo interpretive piece 'No-one Likes Me Anymore' waltz, which is always a particularly emotional one for all involved.

The most dramatic performances of 'You Have No Idea What It's Like' follow early and emotional recitals of the powerful 'My Heart Is Broken', a difficult dance that unfortunately everyone will endure at least once in their lives and in my experience is especially popular with 13–19 year olds.

Following their particular choice of opening number, the teenager will engage in a game of cat and mouse with the parents, avoiding questions such as "Are you sure you're OK?", by simply responding in monosyllabic mutterings.

At this point the parent will offer nuggets of wisdom from their own experience of an extensive teenage dance repertoire. This advice, based on the assumption that they 'know exactly what it's like' because 'this happened to me when I was younger', will be immediately rejected, often prompting one or both parents to repeat the same advice again in a slightly more insistent tone. This routine is repeated until the final movement is reached and the teenager will seek to escape the dance floor with a parting move, performed loudly and with feeling . . .

"You have no idea what it's like to be me."

It is important to remember that this may not be the exact phrase used. It is also acceptable for teenage dancers to conclude the performance with 'You just don't understand' or 'You're not actually listening to what I'm saying', accompanied by a satisfying, if ultimately pointless, door slam for a big finish.

I'm going to go out on a limb here and suggest that these scenarios might be familiar to you?

Now you're beginning to understand, let me ask you a question,

How good a dancer are you?

Patterns

FANCY A COFFEE?

These are just two of many, many dances we perform in our families and we get stuck in them because each and *every* human being has one thing in common. We all have a brain.

In the most basic terms, the brain is a decision making machine and, to make our daily decisions, it needs energy. In fact, it is estimated that the average human brain, while only about 2% of your body mass, consumes over 20% of your daily energy intake, even at rest.[2] That's a hungry wee monkey you have there in your head.

This might explain why our mood is affected when we are tired, stressed, haven't eaten properly or when anything else affects our energy. Your mind has a priority list of where and how your energy will be distributed and if there's not enough fuel being supplied in the form of food, water, sleep etc., priority is given to keeping your heart beating and your muscles working. Your brain will be limited in the amount of energy it is allowed and, once that happens, concentration, focus and decision-making become a lot more difficult.

Because your brain is hungry it is also designed to be hugely efficient. Your mind doesn't want to have to think if it doesn't have to.

For instance, if you drink tea or coffee, what do you take in it?

I would guess you didn't have to think about that for very long! The answer was just there and it has been the same answer for as long as you can remember. This is how our mind works efficiently

---

[2] Drubach, D. *The Brain Explained*. New Jersey: Prentice-Hall, 1999.

– it creates repetitive patterns which means it doesn't have to think any more than it needs to.

Your mind is confident that if you do the same thing, the same way, with the same components then you *should* get the same end result every single time.

And most of the time, it's absolutely right.

You put the required amounts of sugar, milk and hot water into your tea or coffee and you are pretty much guaranteed to enjoy the resultant beverage.

However, what if an extra sugar, a little bit of extra milk or even a spoonful of honey in your tea would make it taste even better?

What if you came round to my place and I made you a cup of tea – I asked you how you usually like it and then I said, "Just to let you know, I put a chopped jalapeño pepper in your tea because I thought you were looking a bit tense and needed to try something new today"?

You'd be pretty pissed off because you really wanted a cup of tea and didn't need me messing with it!

As humans we love patterns and dislike deviation from those patterns. We know what we know, we like what we like, we know what we like and we like what we know. What we don't like is anything or anyone to tell us differently, especially when our emotions are on edge.

And that's a problem when you're a teenager.

As a teen, you are a hormonal soup for nearly 8 years. Your emotions are often, if not always, on edge and you haven't yet learned any patterns that can effectively and quickly switch them off.

And that's a problem when you're a parent.

As a parent, you are *living* with this hormonal soup for nearly 8 years. Their teenage emotions have a direct impact on your emotions which often, if not always, puts you on edge and, for some reason, none of your old patterns can effectively and quickly switch them off. That's why you try and turn the teen emotions off instead.

And that's a problem when you're a teenager.

For quite literally all of your life, your parents have known how to help. Now they seem to want to control you, tell you what to do and treat you like a child when you're not. You can feel that you are quickly becoming an adult and you need your own space and the trust to make your own decisions and mistakes.

Then again . . . you also need them to be there for you when you mess up. But *only* when you need them to be! You don't want them interfering . . .

And that's a problem when you're a parent.

As a parent you will ask yourself, "Why won't they listen when I'm only trying to help?". You want to step back and let them grow but they are making mistakes all over the place and you've done pretty well at helping them for the last 13+ years, why won't they just let you guide them now?

Especially since you remember how bad it felt when you messed up as a teenager. You don't want them to make the same mistakes you did and you are certain that you 'know exactly what it's like'.

Uh-oh, there's that phrase again!

And this, right here, is *how* we dance.

LOOKING UNDER THE HOOD

We dance because that is what we have learned to do. It is our 'normal'.

All of our patterns and dances feel comfortable because, over time, we have found that they work well for us. In fact they work so well for us, we often have trouble understanding why everyone else doesn't just do what we do.

"Why do you do it that way when you can do it my way? I've been doing it my way for years now. It really works."

But when you are really honest, do all your patterns actually work or are you just doing what you've always done?

We refuse a jalapeño in our tea not just because we think it's going to be horrible (although it probably will be) but because we are not used to it.

Remember when people started to regularly add savoury flavours to sweet things? When salt was first added to caramel, everyone thought it was the most crazy, ridiculous thing they'd ever heard. Then people started chucking chilli and beetroot and other crazy things into chocolate. And then putting chocolate into cheese. The world had gone *truly* mad!

But actually it's not really all that far away from a jalapeño in your tea. Way back, before the days of savoury and sweet combos, we simply weren't used to it. Now these flavour combinations are commonplace and are, therefore, considered the new 'normal'.

You see, our concept of normal isn't static. Normal is always moving. Normal is just what we have become used to.

Your normal for tea may be milk and two sugars now but that doesn't mean that it has always been that way or that it always will be.

Your normal weekday routine may be that you get up at 7:30am to get to work on time. But if you were to move house or change job that will change and you will make a new 'normal'.

Your normal may be that your child should agree with your decisions and be obedient. But your teen is training to be an adult and you should consider whether it is normal for a grown man or woman to agree with everything their parents say?

Your normal is changing.

People think their own particular brand of normality is 'right' and that's what keeps the world interesting . . . in most cases there is no 'right'. There is only what works for you.

As teens and parents, all we can do in life is make the best decisions we can with the knowledge we have. Your mind, like the one that drives your teenager, is a state of the art piece of equipment needed to access that knowledge. However, very few people really know how to use it and struggle even more when it comes to knowing how to positively influence someone else's.

And this is *why* we dance.

It's only when we take the time and make the effort to learn more about how our minds work that we can turn the dance into something more useful.

THE EQUIPMENT

There are three main ways people think they can make any problem go away:

1. They try to make everything better by removing the perceived cause of the problem.
2. They try and force the problem to go away by offering benefits for change or threatening consequences for staying the same.
3. They use some form of distraction to alleviate the emotional symptoms of the problem in the hope it will just go away on its own.

Let's try an example that may be familiar to you – a teenager who refuses to disengage from technology when it's time to go to bed. As a parent, you might:

1. Turn off the wifi in the house.
2. Offer a treat if they do what you want or threaten to take away their phone/tablet if they don't.
3. Encourage them to read or find something else to do instead.

Sometimes these approaches do work or at least *appear* to work at first. But in most cases, they are quick fixes, destined to fail in the long term. Yet almost all of our parenting strategies are built on some variation of them. This, at first glance, may seem odd. Surely as sensible adults we would notice if our strategies weren't effective?

But we don't. And there's actually a good reason why.

Remember, we are all decision making machines.

Every routine, every pattern, every dance, every single thing we do whether we think it is 'normal' or not, begins with a decision. But a split second before that decision, something needs to happen to make us decide how we are going to respond or react. This something is called the *trigger*.

In that split second, our minds will subconsciously recall *all* our previous experiences of that particular trigger and will use that information to help us decide what our normal response will be.

Do we like it? Do we not like it? Are we scared of it? Do we fight it? Do we run away from it? Does it make us angry? Does it make us happy?

What is important to remember though is that our responses are *not* produced by the trigger itself. Our response is produced by our *thoughts about* whatever the trigger may be.

Does that make sense?

If I ask you how you like your tea, your mind will access previous tea drinking experiences, allowing you to decide how to respond.

How does it do that? Simple, it gives you a feeling.

If I tell you I'm going to put a chopped jalapeño in your tea, you will get some sort of feeling that this isn't normal. This feeling represents your mind differentiating between what *is* normal for you (tea with milk and two) and the current reality (tea with chilli peppers).

In this case (for most people at least) the mind will recognise that jalapeño tea is not the expected reality and this tea, given all it knows, will be less enjoyable than your usual tea. This feeling leads to the decision that it should be avoided.

This is of course a very basic example, but it is true to say that in any scenario where your reality falls short of your expectation, the gap between the two will be filled by a negative feeling. This feeling may be confusion, anger, sadness, disgust, fear, disappointment or a combination.

However, if the new reality should exceed your expectation of what is 'normal', this gap will be filled with a positive emotion such as contentment, excitement, happiness, joy, love or some other positive feeling.

Now think about the last time you felt a strong emotion (negative or positive) toward your teenager. Notice how that emotion filled the gap between your expectation of them and what actually happened in reality.

Maybe you were disappointed because you expected your teenager to behave in a certain way and in reality they behaved differently.

Or perhaps something more positive ... maybe you were filled with pride because your teenager performed above and beyond in some activity and showed you that they were much more than you thought they could be.

These feelings, both negative and positive, are important because it's our feelings that drive us to make decisions and help us get stuff done! How would you know what to do in any situation if you didn't know how you felt?

It actually boils down to a very simple process that can be summarised like this,

Trigger > Thought > Feeling > Action

Now, I'm not going to go in to too much depth about this process here because that's already been covered elsewhere.[3] What's important is that we gain a clear understanding of how we can make the process work for us, especially when we are interacting with others.

TOTALLY TRIGGERED

As a general rule we, and by 'we' I mean all of us, have a terrible habit (aka a *pattern*) of blaming anything/anyone other than ourselves for how we feel.

Adults blame the weather, their partners, the government, the kids, the newspapers, the dog, the colour of the living room wallpaper and a whole heap of other external factors as reasons for things in our life not being the way we want them to be.

As a teenager we tend to focus on things like our teachers, hormonal changes, our group of friends, people outside our group of friends, the dog, anyone more than 10 years older than us, the pressures of social media, exams and a host of other things which are all easy, external targets for any fragile emotional state.

On some occasions we are right; sometimes it really *was* the dog but, as you're about to discover, more often than not, the real cause of the way we feel is much, much closer to home.[4]

---

[3] My first book *Breakthrough: A Blueprint For Your Mind* covers this process in more detail. See www.rcbks.com/breakthrough

[4] For balance, we should say here that we also blame the world for the good stuff that happens in our lives too. We attribute the source of our success to luck, or someone else's efforts, or the alignment of the stars and never really stop to acknowledge and recognise the amazing things that we have actually done to make this success happen.

When our idea of 'normal' is broken, we will rarely look to ourselves as the problem straight away. When we feel bad, the first thing we want to find is the *cause*, a reason, a 'why?'.

We ask "What is it that could possibly have caused me to no longer feel 100% happy? It's quite obviously nothing to do with me. I didn't choose to feel as bad as I do, why would I do that? That would be totally nuts. There must be a reason why this has happened and, since it definitely isn't my fault, then I'm going to find out who or what is to blame and I'm going to shout at it . . . a lot."

The 'why' doesn't even need to make any real logical sense, it just needs to be feasible.

Imagine a teenager has big exams looming and is procrastinating about studying. They *want* to study, and say they are *trying* to study, but ultimately they don't do enough. When the exams come around, disaster ensues. The teenager feels disappointment, embarrassment, anger, frustration and a whole host of other emotions.

To any external observer, the disaster was clearly caused by procrastination but, because of the way the mind works, that's not how our teenager is going to process it. On the hunt for a cause, they are sure of only one thing – it was definitely, 100%, absolutely nothing to do with them!

Some likely responses that I hear often when talking to teenagers in this situation,

"The teachers didn't teach us properly."
"My parents didn't push me enough/pushed me too hard."
"The exam was too hard."
"No-one told me what to study."
"I didn't want to do it anyway/only doing it because my parents wanted me to."

. . . and the list goes on and on and on.

And, as you well know, parents aren't immune to this either! Similar scenarios can unfold in countless circumstances, most commonly from some household chore that should have been completed years ago. The fact that it has not been completed is, of course, not your fault at all but rather due to a lack of time, a poorly stocked DIY store, lack of decent weather or even simply a bad memory!

In both of these examples, the feelings of inadequacy experienced are blamed on the circumstances and people around us, over which we have little or no control.

But that's not true because

Trigger > Thought > Feeling > Action

Feelings are not caused by triggers; they are caused by the *thoughts* about the triggers.

And you are in control of your thoughts. Even if you don't realise you are.

Neither you, nor your teenager, are emotional pinball machines, continually being triggered by words, circumstances, actions and people. You both have many more choices than that – the circumstances and people around us are simply convenient scapegoats for our feelings.

The harsh reality is that when you are pointing fingers at anyone or anything telling them to change to help you feel better, you are pointing at the wrong place. If you are really ready for change then it's time to realise something very, very important.

It's not them. It's *you*.

The issue is not the circumstances you are in; it's the way you *respond* to the circumstances. And the first step towards long term change is to accept that you have a choice over how you respond to the world around you.

Making that choice isn't always easy and, in almost every situation you will ever face throughout your life, it is made unconsciously. That's why we often don't realise the choice has been made until it is too late and we have already exploded, broken down, run away or whatever it is that we do when things don't go our way.

This might make more sense if we expand our summary a little,

Trigger > Thought > Feeling > *Decision* > Action

The feelings produced by your thoughts about the trigger drive your actions via a decision that you make and this is where you have a choice.

And here's the key . . .

the action you decide to take does not have to reflect the feeling you have.

If you are aware of the process that is happening in your mind, you have the ability to make better choices.

If you are angry, you can still choose to act calmly.

If you are disappointed, you can still choose to be supportive.

If you are excited, you can still choose to reign in unrealistic expectations.

And it's not just actions. The words you choose to use can have an enormous effect on how a conversation or situation progresses. More of that later . . .

It's important to say, I am not suggesting that every argument in your house is your fault and the only way to deal with it by changing the way you respond. Sometimes a teenager (or an adult!) does something that is quite clearly wrong, bad, nasty or disrespectful and that needs to be dealt with firmly.

Such (hopefully infrequent) situations aside, I'm asking you to look at the process more closely and consider if your approach could change and what effect that would have.

Are you allowing the emotion(s) that you bring to the situation to overwhelm your ability to deal with it?

DEVILS AND ANGELS

Of course when we realise that pointing fingers doesn't make us feel better for more than a few minutes, do we learn from our mistakes and stop?

Oh no. We're nowhere near that smart!

As you sit here, calmly reading this book, you already know that if you point your finger at someone in your house and scream "IT'S YOUR FAULT I'M ANGRY", it doesn't really do much to take away your anger. I mean, you're still angry and now, because emotions are contagious, you've infected someone else with your emotions and now they are angry and emotional too!

And you also know that this is only the start of the dance. The original issue that angered you isn't likely to change just because you shouted at someone about it.

The reality is that you are no further forward in discovering a satisfactory resolution.

Then what do we do? Well, at this stage many of us try a new tactic. One we use on ourselves and on other people frequently without even realising that we are doing it . . .

Pleasure and Pain

As a parent, every time money is offered to pass an exam, fast food for tidying a room, a material prize for doing/trying/winning, we are employing one of the oldest motivational tricks in the book.

As a teen, every time mum or dad are told that they are the best mum or dad in the world, or an offer is made to do/try/study/win something in return for a material prize or a promise that the dishes will be done if only they are allowed to do something or go somewhere it's exactly the same, age-old strategy in action.

These are all simple and familiar examples of the *pleasure* approach. However, most of us have learned from experience that *pain* can also be an effective path to motivation.

In most families, we find that both parents and teens use pain much more often than pleasure. We seem to have an inherent understanding that in many cases it is more effective than pleasure but, much more importantly, it also becomes our *pattern*.

Removal or refusal of access to something important, the threat of a bad mood, raised voice or other punishment, bad dancing in public causing widespread family embarrassment (one of my personal favourites that one) are all threats of potential pain. All of them can be used just as effectively as pleasure to motivate a family member to do something they are currently not doing or to stop doing something that they are.

Pain is also the motivational tactic we most often use on ourselves.

Pain is our 'normal'.

For example, which of these statements do you think people use more often to motivate themselves to diet?

"I love myself dearly and I think I can look even more fabulous than I do right now. I deserve to do the best for myself."

or

"Oh no, look at the state of me. I am so disgusting, I can't believe I've let myself go this far and I've become such a big, fat, greasy slob."

It doesn't take much to figure out that there are far more people living in fear, anxiety and worry about failure and not living up to expectation than there are living in confidence, pride and contentment about the possibility of future success, love and fulfilment.

Now, on the face of it, both approaches, pleasure and pain, would seem to work.

They bring a sense of achievement to a parent because they generate an instant response and make stuff happen. For example, in my family, I know that *either* the threat of a public dad-dancing display *or* the offer of an evening out at the cinema are both effective ways of making things happen.

Sort of.

It depends on how we define 'effective'.

They are both based on some sound psychology, that's for sure. Pleasure and pain are powerful motivators but they only work for a brief period and, annoyingly, you can never fully control which direction the motivation is going to go!

How many times do you need to reward the doing of, or punish the avoiding of, washing the dishes before you realise that you aren't actually changing anything? It still won't be done if you don't ask. You are merely motivating a short term change in behaviour by offering the reward (pleasure) or administering the punishment (pain).

How often have you threatened to go nuts if their room isn't tidied? How's that going for you? Working well? I take it that after all these years your repeated bad moods and shouting have created long term behavioural change and your teen now displays a perfect room cleaning routine where even the curtain rail is wiped down at least once a month?

No?

Really?

And I bet most teenagers will recognise that the tactic of losing their temper, going off in a huff, slamming a door or making their parents' lives just a little more difficult, very rarely changes their parents' mind on something. In fact, on most occasions, trying to administer pain to a parent will actually have the opposite effect entirely.

I would suggest that none of us, parents nor teens, really *want* this to be the way things go.

It doesn't matter if it's pleasure or pain, whether it's shouting, slamming, grounding or whatever it is we do, all of these things only make us feel better for moments in time.

These short term tactics only give us a brief glimpse of change and too often, we think we have no alternative, we just do the same things over again and again.

Shouting, Praising, Rewarding, Punishing
Rewarding, Punishing, Praising, Shouting
Praising, Shouting, Punishing, Rewarding

And the process repeats . . .

Manipulating someone into changing will produce short term results but very quickly both teens and parents will get tired of the same tactics being used over and over again.

However, there is a way to motivate long term lasting change and it's easy to do. The only problem is that we are often just too *stuck* to go there.

THE CLOAK OF INVISIBILITY

Any pattern, repeated often enough, will become diluted in importance and will eventually just be ignored.

It will become 'normal' and the effects of the pattern become invisible.

As an example, how often do you really pay attention to your regular daily commute? You do the same things, at the same time, in the same order every day and probably only really notice them when something affects your usual routine. Maybe you slept in, the train was late, the traffic lighter/heavier than usual or your regular coffee shop was closed when you got there.

On a normal day you don't really notice that you get up with your alarm, the train is on time, the traffic flow is about normal and the coffee shop open as usual. You *delete* these facts from your consciousness because anything that is repeated often enough is liable to become familiar to the extent that it is simply not noticed.

In the same way, the use of pleasure and pain is a concept that the mind finds all too familiar. And with this familiarity, comes deletion and therefore immunity to their effects.

Rewards are no longer big enough, shouting is no longer loud enough, door slamming and going off in a huff becomes 'just what you always do', familiar compliments lose their power in overuse and regular insults become just words that are easy to ignore.

If we try a *pain* tactic and don't see an action, our mind deduces that this approach has obviously not worked. We might consider a switch to a *pleasure* tactic or we just might turn up the pain. If nothing happens then we might turn it up some more . . . and more and more until we get that reaction we have been waiting for. In our minds, this is the only outcome that indicates our tactic has 'worked'.

And that means rewards are withdrawn, shouting becomes even louder, compliments are forgotten and insults become nastier.

How loud/painful/provocative do you need to be to provoke a response and get a reaction?

And can you be sure that you will get the response or reaction you are hoping for?

If we use a *pleasure* tactic, it often goes the opposite direction. We give the compliment or the reward and, if there is no action or response, we can't understand why there are not somersaults of gratitude and conclude that the target of all our generosity obviously doesn't care. Therefore, we end the *pleasure* hoping that this will be a way to cause *pain* and the cycle begins again.

We are stuck in a loop.

BREAKING THE PATTERNS

On the face of it, it might seem impossible to break these patterns of behavior. I promise it's not impossible . . . but it might be difficult.

And only because it's new.

Think back to the first time you ever did anything new. Didn't it feel a bit weird?

We question new ways of behaving because they are simply not what we are used to. When someone proposes something that doesn't seem to make logical sense, we feel that it will be difficult and it's all too easy to dismiss it as 'impossible'.

It's not impossible, it just feels difficult because it's new. And that's OK.

I remember, just couple of years ago, standing at the top of a very large, snowy (indoor) hill with an artistically decorated plank of moulded wood strapped to my feet, my heart racing and my backside aching from some very frequent bumps!

I had spent the last hour 'enjoying' my first ever snowboard lesson during which I had been falling over, a lot, because my mind thought that it knew better than my instructor! I was finding it very hard to override my own patterns of thought and behaviour to try something new, something that didn't feel natural. The more I resisted it, the more I fell over and the more it hurt.

You see, to slow down while riding a snowboard, you lean forward, pushing onto your front foot. If you want to rattle down a hill really quickly then lean back, lifting the front of the snowboard off the ground and this will cause you to go a lot faster.

But my mind, with all its established patterns told me, 'If I'm going down a hill and I want to slow down, I lean back. That is logical and what I am used to. When I walk, or run down a hill, I lean back to slow down, and that's what I'm going to do on this snowboard, I'll lean baaaaa . . .'

This thought process was inevitably cut short by a painful thump and deep gratitude for my helmet.

And that's how I found myself stuck in the Dance of the Bruised Backside, leaning back to slow down and finding myself picking up speed! Then, to compensate for how fast I am hurtling down the hill, I lean back further, sticking to my old pattern, pushing weight onto my back foot, find myself going even faster and then falling over in a spectacular, painful snowy tumble.

I couldn't change my old established patterns in this new set of circumstances and they continued to cause me pain.

All too often our mind thinks it knows the right answer when it quite clearly doesn't. Even when the result causes us emotional or physical pain, we find it hard to trust ourselves or other people enough to try something new. We remain stuck in rigid patterns and continue hurting ourselves, and those we love, over and over again.

But when we trust enough to change . . . that's when magic can happen.

I love snowboarding and I rarely fall over now, largely because I learned to trust my instructor's advice that leaning forward will slow me down. The first time I did it, I will admit, my heart was pounding and my mind was telling me that it was all going to go wrong and I was going to hurt myself.

But that didn't happen.

I slowed down, controlled the ride, got to the bottom of the hill still standing upright and my brain began learning a new 'normal'. A normal that would not have worked if I had been running down the hill, was perfect for keeping me safe as I slid down it on my artistically decorated plank.

Now it's automatic and I don't even think about how to lean. It just happens. I see learners on the hill falling over and hurting themselves just like I did and I can understand what is happening – they are stuck in their old 'normal'.

Trusting yourself, or others, to change patterns of thought and behavior isn't easy especially when your mind wants to keep doing things that don't work. But it's not impossible. It's just not easy.

Once you begin to see things differently, you will begin to understand that your experiences have taught you many flawed lessons.

PSYCHOLOGICAL JUDO

You may think that some of the dances you see your family perform are ridiculous. You may even think some of them are dangerous, awkward, infuriating and a little crazy. I guarantee, the rest of your family are thinking *exactly* the same about your dances!

As we discussed earlier, our natural reaction to behaviour we don't understand is to use the strategies of pleasure and pain, when actually the first steps to defeating negative behaviour should be to accept, understand and trust yourself to try something new.

I want to give you one invaluable insight into the workings of the mind that I believe makes the difference between someone who is 'reactive' to the world around them and someone who 'responds' to the world around them.

Every pattern of behaviour exists for a positive reason.

The mind operates with the sole aim of ensuring the safety, protection and happiness of its owner. Every single pattern of thought, behaviour and action created by your mind is there because, on some level, it helps you. There is a positive intention at the core of everything we do, even if and when it causes pain. And we can learn to understand this, absorb the force of the pain and use it to our advantage – just like in judo.

In judo, victory does not rely on strength but in skillfully using the energy and momentum of your opponent against them. Absorbing their physical attack by moving with it will often be a far more effective strategy than brute strength or head on attack. Understanding and predicting the direction of your opponent will allow you to turn their efforts to your advantage.

If someone is procrastinating, self harming, depressed, anxious, angry, withdrawn or indulging in any other negative emotional behavior, they are doing what they are doing because, on some level, their mind believes it is helpful.

Yes, it might sound weird, but trust me, it's absolutely true!

One of the first keys to cracking the teen code is to get as close as you can to understanding what that positive reason may be *before you respond*.

Let's use a common example.

Let's imagine you discover your teen has started smoking. You instantly and correctly decide that this has to stop and you also decide a *pain* approach is necessary to scare them into action. As your teenager walks in the door from school one day, you are ready to confront them.

In a voice approaching the volume of a jet engine, you inform your teenager how disappointed you are. You make sure to tell them in no uncertain terms just how it ruins their body and causes cancer, how bad it is for their health in other ways, how expensive it is, how it makes you stink and how you can't believe someone with all their intelligence could be so stupid. You ridicule their friends who are obviously a bad influence and you immediately withdraw all sources of money and confine your teen to the house for the next 4 weeks.

Pain has been administered.

Sound reasonable?

I believe many parents would agree with this approach. But if you look at it again and think about the psychology of change that we have discussed already in this chapter, how would you rate this pain-orientated approach in terms of its ability to create immediate and long lasting change?

I suspect you said very low. And you'd be absolutely right. Why? Well, that's easy . . .

Every pattern of behaviour exists for a positive reason.

No-one starts smoking (or any of the other myriad of bizarre teen behaviour that we mentioned earlier) by accident. There's no moment where a teen says 'oops I didn't *mean* to try that cigarette, it just kind of popped into my mouth already lit'. There is always a positive reason that is the motivation behind the behavior. So how do we find this reason?

As a parent, you can try shouting "you're being stupid and so are your friends, I expected more from you" or you can try crying "you've let me and this whole family down". You can even try the cold shoulder "don't even talk to me about it, you make your own choices and they are nothing to do with me" approach but the thing you have to notice with all these approaches is that in each one it ends up being about the parent,

"I expected more"

"you've let me down"

"[your choices] are nothing to do with me (even if I am acting like they totally are anyway.)"

In reality, this has absolutely nothing to do with you, the parent. When your teen started smoking, their intention was not to do it to hurt you. But, when you adopt an approach that makes it about you rather than about them and their motivations, you have missed an opportunity for change.

Chinese Finger Traps are 6–7 inch long tubes of colourful, wicker like material and are perfectly finger sized. They are one of my favourite tools. I hand these out frequently at workshops, ask the delegates to place a finger in each end of the tube until they are firmly held by the device and, once they are comfortable, I simply ask them to remove their fingers.

On the face of it this sounds like it should be easy but if you've ever tried one you will know, in reality, it's anything but easy. Perhaps the clue is in the name . . .

It's a trap!!

The harder you pull, the tighter the trap grips. This tends to surprise the unfortunate subject and cause them to pull even harder which, in turn, causes the grip to tighten further! The more our 'victim' pulls, the more stuck they become.

The next time you are tempted to try to drag someone kicking and screaming away from something that they believe, on some level, is helping them, remember the Chinese Finger Trap and understand the harder you pull, the tighter the grip becomes.

One day, I hope to have the pleasure of seeing your fingers stuck in this flimsy little tube of bamboo at one of my courses. For that reason I won't give the solution away here, though I will say that to begin the process of freedom you first of all have to relax.

And that is the key to change.

Before you confront your smoking teenager, relax and ask yourself, calmly and rationally *why* are they doing what they are doing? What could possibly be the biggest positive they get from smoking?

Remember the Two Teen Questions:

Who am I? and **How do I fit in?**

Perhaps this behaviour has started because they want to fit in and be accepted? Or because they want to stand out from the crowd? Or because they are stressed or anxious and they need something that calms their mind and distracts them? Or because they are bored and need something to do to make them feel excited or stimulated?

It could be any of these and a million other reasons but when you find the reason, *accept* it, *understand* it and you can use it as the stimulus for change.

Think about other ways they might be accepted, other ways to calm themselves when they are stressed, other ways to stimulate their senses and other ways to stand out from the crowd.

I'm not promising that your active acceptance and understanding will immediately make your teen come round to your way of thinking and stop smoking there and then. I'm also not saying that you should sit back passively and not mention your feelings on their new habit.

Taking the time to understand someone's motivation for any behaviour will always make it more possible that you can help them change it.

For example, if you can identify all the places that your newly smoking teen *isn't* fitting in, the friends they have *lost* due to their new habit, the fact they now have to hang about outside in the rain and cold when *everyone else is inside enjoying themselves*.

You can use that as leverage.

That's 'pain' used properly.

STIRRING THE SOUP

However, even knowing all you now know, *delivery* is everything.

Let me ask you how you respond to family crisis?

Are you a shouter? A pacifier? A placater? A clown? A rewarder? A punisher?

And why do you keep using the same approach, even in those moments when it clearly isn't working and nothing is changing?

I've heard many answers to this question but by far the most common is 'I do it because I love them and I want the best for them'.

With that in mind let me ask another of my favourite parent questions – do you think your teenager experiences and feels your love when you respond in the way you do?

For example . . . "I'M ONLY SHOUTING AT YOU BECAUSE I LOVE YOU".

Honestly, seeing through your teen's eyes, do you think your teen feels your love and acceptance in that moment? Or do they see anger, disappointment and maybe even hatred?

Or what about the opposite . . . "You make your own choices in life. You do what you have to do and I'm sure it will all work out OK."

Does your teen see that you are looking to give them responsibility and trust? Or does it just come across like you don't care and that you think nothing they do will make them happy?

Can I suggest it might be easier to show it another way?

For these few years, when our kids are experiencing huge change and one of the most intense periods of emotional vulnerability they will ever have in their lives, they need to know at least that you are on their side.

Make *what* you are doing a reflection of *why* you are doing it.

Then just maybe, they might do the same.

If you want to show love then act like someone who loves. If you're angry then by all means show that too, but make the outside a reflection of the inside and be angry *and* loving. I promise that is possible. It's your decision to make.

If we are honest, no-one likes their 'normal' being broken. In most circumstances I would go as far as to say we fight it at every turn. We say we don't like change but that's not really true. Our brains are designed to be adaptive, always learning, refining and making things easier. If we are always learning that means we are always changing.

We just don't want to change too much!

As we have seen, we don't like anything too far away from 'normal'. Small changes are ok but please don't take me too far away from my version of comfortable and safe.

With this in mind I'm hoping it's starting to make sense as to why it is that both you and your teenager may sometimes ignore common sense and continue to do stupid stuff that doesn't work!

I hope this is also explaining why your broken Family Dances continue.

In moments of clarity and calm, you *say* things will be different next time but, if we're being honest (and we are always being honest here) doing it differently is easier said than done.

When you step back and begin to recognise the dances, the patterns and all the ineffective ways of thinking and acting that you and your family have made normal, you are already one step closer to cracking the teen code.

We can do it one small change at a time.

As parents, I believe we have one job during the difficult teenage years. We are a guide to growing up, an assistant to our teens as they search for the answers to the Two Teen Questions,

Who am I? and **How do I fit in?**

There will be mistakes along the way. Did you always clean your room when you were asked? Were you ever unreasonable, frustrated or angry as your hormonal soup caused your emotions to be raw and exposed? Did you ever hurt the people you loved the most, intentionally or otherwise?

When you were a teen, you had your own dances with your own parents and I guarantee you performed them regularly. Maybe now that you are a parent you even find yourself on the opposite side of some familiar routines from the past!

Influencing the causes of our behaviours by pleasure and pain is short term thinking. Real change happens when we step back from an issue that is repeating and choose not to dance anymore.

And the very first step to change is to notice there is an issue in the first place because put quite simply,

you can't change a problem you don't know you have.

If you don't see your behaviour, actions or responses as a problem, why would you change them?

Once you have accepted that at least some of the issue lies with you, you can start to do something about it. You can acknowledge that you can change it, and begin to understand that it doesn't have to go the way it always has.

And at this early stage, that's more than enough to ask for.

TIME TO LEAN FORWARD

Here's a new thing to try if you want to break some of the patterns in your house. What I'm about to suggest will feel strange, alien and sometimes even wrong but please give it a proper go and stick with it. No half hearted attempts, if you read on and choose to do this then you must promise to commit to it for at least a few days.

Ready?

Your pattern-breaking challenge is to . . .

do the complete *opposite* of what you've been doing up to now.

If you normally shout, say absolutely nothing.

If you usually say nothing, start saying it how it is.

If you offer frequent rewards, don't.

If you believe that whatever it is should just be done, then start at the very least complimenting if not rewarding any good behaviour you witness.

If you usually fight back, start listening, understanding and being attentive.

If you always try to be the understanding one, start saying when you think they are talking nonsense.

Whatever you are doing that isn't working, stop and do something different.

And as you do that, you start to notice how to break the next stage of the Code.

Chapter 2 – What The . . . ?

- Every family dances. A family that wants to change needs to begin spotting the dances that don't work any more.

- Remember, it's not always them – sometimes it's you. Some of the dances that need to change might be yours.

- *Every* thing that we do, think and feel is there for a positive reason. Find that reason and you have a key to change.

- Pleasure and Pain are short term solutions. You need to think like a human and less like a parent!

- Change takes trust and will sometimes be scary. Lean forward, give it a shot, see what happens.

- Pay attention. If what you do isn't working, do the opposite and take it from there.

3

To Infinity and Beyond

Buzz Lightyear is a total arsehole.

He arrives in Andy's room believing he is a Space Ranger, a heroic officer of Star Command protecting the world against the evil Emperor Zurg who threatens our world with his dastardly, megalomaniac ways.[1] But, in reality, Buzz is just a lump of moulded plastic.

Despite frequently being told that he is not a Space Ranger and is in fact nothing more than a toy, he refuses to listen. Buzz holds on to his unshakeable self confidence and mistaken belief that he is a Space Ranger because there seems to be, at least to him, a complete lack of evidence to the contrary.

He believes he can fly, he believes he is surrounded by evidence of alien invasion and he also believes that everyone around him is merely a barrier to completing his mission.

Buzz's mistaken belief in who he is leads a close knit group of friends through an adventure filled with anger, mistrust, arguments, and upset that none of them really wanted to go on.

Basically, he's just a total arsehole!

But in many ways, I admire him.

---

[1] *Toy Story*. Dir. John Lasseter. Disney/Pixar, 1995.

It's good to have confidence and not listen to people who try and pull you down and tell you that you can't be all you want to be. It's good to have a high opinion of yourself and believe you have the personal power to create change. It's good to have a strong sense of who you are and what you can achieve and, with all of these positive characteristics, I could argue that Buzz is completely justified in his unshakeable self belief . . . but I'd be wrong.

You see, we have something that Buzz doesn't. We have access to all the evidence.

We can see that he's wrong but only, and this is important, because we know things that he doesn't.

We can see the trouble he is creating for himself and all the people around him.

We can see that he can't really fly and that his laser is just a small, red light.

We can see that he is a toy.

But Buzz can't.

He doesn't have all the evidence. He only has what he has been programmed to know.

When you look at it like that, we can all be a little bit Buzz Lightyear sometimes.

WHICH BOX DID YOURS ARRIVE IN?

From the second we are born we are being programmed with information. In our early years, choices are being made about who we will become, what and where we will learn.

For example, you gave your child their name and introduced them to their family. If you follow a particular religion, you more than likely arranged for your children (initially at least) to follow the same one. You will have chosen a school for them to attend. Especially in those first few years, you told them all about how you see the world and what is good, bad and expected of them.

Multiply this process by a teenage number of years and this is how your teenager has learned to be the person they are today.

They weren't born this way, they haven't got a screw loose, they aren't broken, damaged or twisted, they have been expertly taught to be the door slammer/shouter/crier/huffer/fighter/rebel/quiet person or whoever it is that they are.

You programmed them!

Yes, you and many other teachers, taught them *all* that stuff. You didn't think they'd come up with it all on their own, did you?

Let me show you how this works . . .

When I was young I was never a fan of getting hurt. So much so that, rather than take the risk of hurting myself and then having to deal with the pain, I actively sought to avoid any source of potential pain entirely.

Sadly for little Brian, this left a lot of trees unclimbed and ended a potentially glittering rugby career before it ever got started. I did play football and was pretty good but I was never one to enter into any crunching, full blooded tackles – why would I get involved in one of those? I might get hurt!

Fast forward many years and I become a dad. What do you think I inadvertently, but expertly, taught my kids?

I hated the thought of them getting hurt which meant I was always telling them to 'be careful', to 'watch yourself'. I was too quick to give a supporting hand when they climbed a wall or a tree, always wanting to make sure they were safe. I would hold on just that little bit longer then they needed, taking the weight, just to make sure they didn't fall or hurt themselves.

Why?

Because, in my mind, they couldn't possibly be safe without me. If I wasn't there, they might get hurt and to me, getting hurt wasn't a good thing.

And so of course, my girls grew up to be a lot like me. With hindsight, I realise that I spent too much time fussing around them. They could have had many more tree climbing, wall balancing adventures, but I was much happier with them being careful and coming back to me in one piece.

I taught them to be careful. And now, as they enter adulthood, they are still careful. But neither of my daughters were *born* physically cautious. This is one of the many things that my wife and I have unwittingly programmed into their personality.

We did it quietly, under the radar, so covertly that even we didn't notice what we were doing until well after the programme had become part of their personality and no longer anything to do with us. By the time I noticed what was happening, they were running the programme themselves and I had lost any influence to change it easily.

Remember how this book started?

Something you do is going to mess your kid up.

This, right here, is how we do it.

This type of personality programming takes years and as a parent you have done it too, 100% guaranteed. In fact, you are still doing it right now. You can't help it!

Now, ask yourself . . . who have you programmed your kids to be?

If programming your children sounds a little too 'robot nation' for you just now, let's imagine you're a chef with a selection of ingredients in your kitchen. You can make many dishes out of these ingredients – some hot, some cold, some sweet, some savoury. It just depends on how you put them all together.

COOKING UP PERFECTION

As an example, one of the most common parental 'recipes' is one of the easiest to follow. In only a couple of years, you can bake a fully-fledged perfectionist. Prepared properly, it will be effective right through to adulthood, can be strengthened on a regular basis and pretty much guarantees the need for therapy at some stage of later life.

Ingredients:
1 child (school age)
1 parent (well meaning)
1 sprinkle parental ambition
1 group of other children, similar age to the main child, school mates or cousins will do nicely
Plenty of opportunities for the main child's performance to be tested and measured

Method:
Take a fresh child and allow him or her to live as normal in almost all areas of their lives. However, unknown to the child a set of

unrealistic standards should be prepared and the child will be asked to live up to these standards daily. For best results, the child should not be made aware of what these standards are.

When opportunity arises for competition, tests or 'getting things right', the parent should remain diligently focused on their child being the 'best', certainly 'as good as everyone else' and never, ever making a mistake. If mistakes should ever occur, the parent must point this out with a delicate mixture of ridicule and disappointment.

During the early years marinating process, be on the lookout for any early perfectionist flavours that become evident in the child, such as excessive frustration at their failure to complete tasks. These simple signs means your perfectionist is coming along nicely – compliments to the chef.

These ingredients should be allowed to gently marinade until the child reaches school age when the full bake can begin in earnest. From this point, and at every opportunity, simply focus on anything the child gets *wrong* rather than what they have right, what has *not* been achieved in preference to what has and use every opportunity to show the child that there is ample room for improvement in every aspect of their performance.

For example,

Child: "Mum, I got 9 out of 10 on the spelling test."
Parent: "Well done! If you'd studied a bit more, maybe you'd have got full marks."

Notice that it is even more effective to criticise the child's performance after softening expectations with a compliment. This causes maximum emotional confusion and ensures you leave the whole situation focused on the negative. In this case, note the addition of 'Well done' as the perfect set up.

Another?

Child: "Dad, I won a silver medal in the (event) at Sports day."
Parent: "Silver's good. But who beat you? Was it (child that always comes first) again?"

Notice again the use of a softener before bringing all the focus to what was *not* achieved rather than what was. In this case, the parent has even taken it a stage further by adding a liberal splash of competition and possibly even a little resentment into the mix.

And as a final example of how to really get the flavour of perfection baked into your children, make them feel inferior by negatively comparing them to someone who meets your approval.

Parent: "Why can't you be more like your brother/sister/friend/cousin?"

As you can see, this ingredient is even easier to apply as it does not require any specific input from the child. Simply with repetition and volume, we can ensure that the message 'You are not as good as this other person' sticks in their mind and causes the maximum amount of long term damage.

If you repeat this program continually for a number of years, around the age of 9 or 10, you will have developed a robust perfectionist. But don't stop there . . . continue to strengthen the recipe into the teenage years and you can make every exam and relationship a struggle of anxiety and pressure for your teen.

Some key signs that your child is a fully baked perfectionist:

- frustration and anger, often aimed at themselves.
- anxiety about any test, challenge or anything where they will be watched or rated.
- a perpetual feeling of being judged.
- anxiety about their looks, weight, intelligence, abilities.
- constant comparison to others.

Any of this sound familiar?

I will admit, I've given an extreme example here, but I want to clearly illustrate that, even with the very best of intentions,

something you do is going to mess your kid up.

I would guarantee some of you read that recipe for a perfectionist, recognised yourself and are now rationalising it in your head to convince yourself that you only want the best for your wee James or Jemima and that you really don't want him/her to be a perfectionist.

Of course you don't! You only want the best for your kids. Doesn't every parent?

A parent that cooks up the 'perfect' perfectionist does so with love and kindness. Their intention is not to cause frustration, anxiety or undue pressure. It's the same with all parental programming.

In the example from my own experience, I only wanted to keep my kids from pain yet now I look on as they struggle to have fun at a waterpark because they fear the slides are too high, too fast or too dangerous.

Remember . . . messing something up does not mean you've done a bad job!!

You've done so much, tried so hard, given all you've got and now, with everything going on for your teen, it can appear to some parents that they have failed, that all that effort has been wasted. Your teen may seem hugely ungrateful for everything you have done and throw it all back at you. If things are really difficult, you may even feel they don't love you, care for you or respect you any more. You may even feel that they hate you.

I have experience of meeting many teens and, while I can't speak for every one of them, I can confidently say that, in most cases, none of these things are true.

In most cases, your teen is just being Buzz.

In those formative years, you taught them everything they needed to know. By the time they reach their teenage years, they think they know how it all works. In their mind, life will always be the way it is now.

For some that will mean striding into the world like Buzz with an over inflated idea of their own importance, thinking they know everything there is to know. For others it will be the complete opposite and the world feels like a terrifying place of danger, ridicule and bullying.

As a teenager, there is a desire to keep everything the same while everything is changing. And remember from the last chapter, we will always resist our version of normal being threatened.

Your child thought they knew who they were and what they wanted from the world but it seems that, as they keep growing up, the world has its own ideas.

FALLING WITH STYLE

While Buzz maintains the illusion that he really is a Space Ranger, he dramatically and unexpectedly falls out of a window and is found by Sid, Andy's extremely unpleasant next door neighbour. In Sid's room, we see the remnants of Sid's toys. Toys he has broken in impossibly horrible ways but Buzz is still blind to the danger he is in. Danger doesn't exist for Buzz, he's a Space Ranger after all.

He is determined to find his way back to his ship. He wants to carry out his mission and save the universe. Woody, who has chased after Buzz to save him from the outside world, gamely tries to convince him that he is a toy but he still won't listen.

And then change happens.

Buzz manages to escape the room of terrifying broken toys, climbs onto a railing at the top of a large flight of stairs, extends his wings and readies himself to heroically fly out the window, return to his ship and continue his mission. He shouts his famous catchphrase "to infinity and beyond" and jumps.

He expects to fly.

He doesn't.

Instead he falls.

He falls a long way.

He hits the ground hard and, amongst other damage, his arm pops off. In this instant, he absorbs a ton of new information, coming to the sudden and stark realisation that he isn't who he thought he was after all. He's just a toy.

Imagine what that must feel like.

Your world changing in one painful, humiliating instant.

Welcome to being a teenager.

As adults, we are guilty of thinking that a miracle happens between the ages of 12 and 19 and our teen will suddenly know how to be an adult. They will know exactly how to behave, how to focus, how to manage their own emotions.

We seem to think that if they *look* like an adult, they should automatically be able to *act* like an adult. But, in truth, the physical self is maturing a lot faster than the emotional self and with a better understanding of what is going on we can start to appreciate why our teens do what they do.

To do that, we need to look into their mind and discuss the Two Teen Questions in more detail.

The Two Teen Questions

Question 1 – "Who Am I?"

CHECK THE LABEL FOR INSTRUCTIONS

As we arrive at our teenage years, we announce who we are by 'wearing' our identity. Suddenly it becomes important to have clothes with slogans, bands, names, brands, colours, symbols and hidden meanings. By how we dress, together with our hairstyle, makeup, piercings and any other external display of individuality, we publicly declare,

'*this is who* I *am*'.

In a similar way, our personal identity on the *inside* is also made up of a mix of labels and badges.

Our internal and external labels and badges combine to define us whether they are given to us by those around us or if we cultivate them ourselves over time. In many cases, they turn out to be completely false representations of who we really are, while in others, they accurately define everything we stand for.

For example, think about a person you really admire and make a list of about six or seven words you would use to describe who they are as a person. Pause your reading just for a minute or two to really consider this little exercise carefully . . . it's important to gain perspective.

Done?

OK, what 'labels' did you use for them?

Caring? Loving? Exciting? Handsome? Ambitious? Extrovert? Introvert? Decisive? Friendly? Well spoken? Sexy? Family orientated?

Energetic? Go-getter? Tall? Short? Fit? Cuddly? Funny? Charitable? Kind? Inspiring? Happy?

These are just a tiny sample of the words we use to label the people in our world. Our ability to 'know' someone, based on our experience of how they look, behave and act is a key component of social awareness.

Just before we move on, let's try the exercise again. This time *you* are the subject.

Think about yourself and make a list of about six or seven words you would use to describe who you are as a person.

Done? I bet that one was more difficult!

If you managed to get any words at all and didn't completely avoid the exercise entirely, how did you describe yourself? Were you kind to yourself, only using positive words as I did in the examples above? Or were there some negatives too?

Angry? Lonely? Frustrated? Sick? Old? Tired? Sad? Short tempered? Control Freak? Pushover? Violent? Victim? Unloved? Not Good Enough? Failure? Lost? Fat? Taken for granted?

Now, think about the list you just used to describe you – do those 'labels' really represent *who you are*? If you used negatives, how does that make you feel about yourself?

Now to complete our labelling exercise, let's consider your teenager. Starting with the negatives. When your teen is doing the things you wish they wouldn't, what labels do you think they would apply to themselves?

Trouble? Bad? Quiet? Liked? Popular? Geek? Man? Woman? Outsider? Goth? Weirdo? Slag? Fat? Dumb? Clown? Nutter? Poison? Bitch?

This is just a small sample of the 'labels' teenagers tend to use to describe themselves and this raises a very important question. Are these 'labels' really what they believe about themselves or are they using a flawed perspective on the world to judge themselves harshly?

During a time of uncertainty i.e. the whole time they are a teenager, it's easy to accept that they must be what people say they are . . . only because this is what people say they are!!

It's not that anyone has come out and called your daughter a bitch or called your son a weirdo but, in passing through the world, your son or daughter have heard people, who's opinions they value, saying 'people that do 'that thing' are bitches' or 'people who like that kind of music/wear those clothes/walk, talk or look like that are weirdos' and that means they must be too.

Does that make sense?

Once we've started down this path, it's easy to allow the labels to shape our behavior and identity, even when they are not a true representation of who we are. We begin to live up to our labels and, by doing so, reinforce them, to the point where they become difficult to shake off.

A common example is the 'trouble maker' who finds academic subjects, like Maths and Science, dull and boring. They get into trouble because they are distracted and can't focus and, before long, the label becomes self-fulfilling and a destructive cycle has begun. All they really want is to have the chance to do something a little less academic and a little more active (may of these kids excel at subjects like woodwork, art and sport) but the school can't or won't offer this. Out of continuing frustration and boredom at being the square peg being forced into the round hole they do things that don't fit the rules – they become 'trouble'. The label sticks, despite being inaccurate, and this becomes how everyone sees them, even how they see themselves.

Jay was 15 when I met him. He was frequently suspended from school and, even when he was there, he was regularly excluded from classes. Because of this, he spent a lot of 'self study' time in the company of teachers who took every opportunity to tell him that he was 'trouble' and 'a lost cause'.

Jay really wanted to show the teachers and his classmates that he wasn't 'trouble' but the label he had been given was well established since the age of 8 or 9. He would argue with teachers when they attempted to discipline him because he felt it was unfair that he was being labeled as 'trouble' when, in his head at least, he really wasn't.

This left him feeling defeated and, the more defeated he felt, the more he just gave up and accepted the 'trouble' label. In his own words, "If they expect me to be trouble all the time then why bother trying to be anything else? They'll only see trouble anyway".

See the problem?

Jay found himself fighting a losing battle because the perception the world had of him was very different from how Jay saw himself.

He labeled himself as 'funny' and said he was a 'nice guy' who just 'wants to be liked'. He had been diagnosed as dyslexic at a relatively late stage and, unfortunately, by the time it was diagnosed, he had already given himself another label – 'stupid'.

When I met him he was long past associating any learning difficulties he had to his dyslexia. As far as he was concerned, probably by comparing himself to those around him, he was just 'stupid' and this caused him a great deal of stress and embarrassment.

He struggled with school work from a very early age, which he thought was because he was 'stupid'. He quickly lost confidence in his academic ability and stopped believing in himself. However, from an early age, he learned that he could distract people from noticing his 'stupidity' by making them laugh and 'being one of the lads'.

This pattern of behaviour worked well for him and made him feel better about himself. When someone or something triggered his 'stupid' label, he hid it by being a clown, making people laugh and proving to himself that he is popular and well-liked. However, in proving his 'popular' label to his peers he was reinforcing his 'trouble' label to his teachers.

And we don't stop there. Of course, when his 'trouble' label was triggered, he fought back against it because if people think he's trouble, they won't like him.

What he couldn't see was that fighting back was compounding the problem.

What the teachers rarely saw was his 'wants to be liked' label being triggered. When this happened people met a different Jay – a genuinely nice guy who wanted to have fun with his pals.

Unfortunately, 'wants to be liked' Jay was so desperate to be liked, he was easily influenced and did all sorts of stupid stuff to fit in. Smoking cigarettes at 12, weed at 13 and frequently drunk, he didn't see a problem because it was ". . . just with my pals."

But it wasn't only his pals that knew about this behaviour, his teachers knew about it too. And what do adults call the class clown who drinks, smokes and doesn't know when to say no?

We call them 'trouble'.

The cycle continued and Jay's search for the answer to the 'Who Am I?' question, led him on a path from which he struggled to break away.

When I met Jay at his school, I felt it was important to help him understand that his identity was *his and his alone* to create and that he had full control of the labels he gave himself and earned from others.

As he began to take responsibility for how he was perceived, he stopped pushing back against the 'trouble' label. He finally understood that fighting back was achieving nothing but negative reinforcement.

In fact, Jay came to realise an important fact of being a grown up human.

We teach other people how to label us.

If you become aware that people consider you an 'angry' person, you need to understand that they aren't just making it up to annoy you! It's because their perception of you is that you are 'angry' and, if you don't like it, *you* need to decide what you are going to do to change it.

Last time I saw Jay he was doing better, making plans to leave school and head to college. His extra curricular activities were still somewhat unhealthy but one step towards a better life is better than none. I know he'd be really chuffed to know that his story is helping you begin to understand your teenager.

And that's the perfect time to ask again; What are your teen's personal labels? If you could be in their head, how do they see themselves?

ARE WE NEARLY THERE YET?

As your teen works their way through the maze of positive and negative labels, you as their parent, are in the perfect position to help them make sense of what is going on.

We have already discussed that acceptance and understanding the motivation behind our teen's behaviour is significantly more powerful than trying to manipulate change using old and ineffective pleasure/pain techniques.

If you want to help and guide your teen, you *need* to know how they see themselves.

I know you have worked hard to nurture and shape a confident young person, filled with self esteem and positivity. And I know you don't yet fully understand why your bright eyed little angel is now locked in their room, wearing black from head to toe, listening to morose music and saying how much they hate the world![2]

Please keep telling them how amazing they are. Please keep telling them how beautiful, handsome, funny, kind and generous they are. Just don't be angry, frustrated or upset when they disagree.

Tell them who they *are*, not who you want them to be. If they aren't academic and are more interested in creative or physical pursuits then this isn't wrong. It's just who they are. Reminding someone

---

[2] Please feel free to replace this example with your own particular flavour of teen drama!

of how far away they are from everything you wanted them to be will create another label I hear often from teenagers – the label of 'disappointment'.

Remember, this is not about you. Your teenager's negative behaviour is not personal. They are not doing what they are doing to upset you, even if that's how it feels. They just don't know who they are yet and, in most cases, they are doing everything and anything they can to find out.

I know this is hard for parents to hear but, if you want to help your teenager grow into the amazing young man or woman you know they can be, accepting and understanding who they are *now* is the way to make change happen.

There's just one small problem . . . who they are now can change frequently, so you'll need to keep up!

To further understand this, let's move on to the second of the Two Teen Questions.

Question 2 – "How Do I Fit In?"

I THINK WE MIGHT BE LOST

Think back to when you were a teenager – who were your biggest influences on how you lived your life and how you made decisions?

Your parents? Actors? Musicians? Politicians? Friends? Sports stars? I suspect the majority of people reading this would answer "all of the above. . .except for my parents!"

For many of us, the thought of sharing a big bunch of labels with our parents is the craziest suggestion anyone could possibly make.

Why would we want to be like them? They're like . . . so out of touch and so . . . old!

And fitting in is all about finding people who share, agree with and even celebrate your labels. So why would any self respecting teen want a label that seems in any way relevant to someone as ancient as 40?

This isn't true of *every* label obviously. Our teens are totally happy to be seen as kind, generous, understanding, clever, friendly and all these personality labels that we, their parents, have instilled in them. It is the outward, superficial labels against which our teens are more likely to rebel.

For example, for many teens, especially in this social media age, being popular, liked and doing what is deemed 'normal' is the best way to fit in. These teens wear the 'right' clothes, go to the 'right' parties, do the 'right' things (which may, to parental eyes, be totally the wrong things) and they find the place where they fit in.

However, others will do the complete opposite, and find their place in an anti-culture based on the antithesis of everything that is 'right' from music to fashion to tattoos and piercings.

This process or fitting in means that it's possible for your teen to become heavily influenced and connected to a specific social circle, defined by a standard set of fashions, musical tastes and behaviours. It's equally possible for them to end up on their own, unable to find anyone with whom they feel as if they share enough labels to be accepted.

There are an infinite number of ways people choose to fit in. The key to having influence over any teenager is to *accept* and *understand* how important fitting in is for them. If you can see the world through this filter of fitting in it will make it so much easier to be there for your teen if, and when, things go wrong.

Because the one certainty of teenage life is that something *is* going to go wrong. It's just a matter of when.

When I meet parents struggling with their teens, many of them can't understand the behaviour they are seeing.

Why would their beautiful baby self harm? Why would their little girl or boy send those photos? Why would their son or daughter need to take drugs to prove himself? Why can't their amazing kid see how they are ruining their future?

And I say the same thing to every one of those parents.

You are thinking about it all wrong.

What they are doing isn't anywhere near as important as *why* they are doing it. You can't change the 'what' without understanding, or at least accepting, the 'why'.

Every pattern of behaviour exists for a positive reason.

Crazy fashion choices, music you can't bear at volumes you can't stand, alcohol, drugs, friends you don't like, swearing, sleeping all the time, lack of care about family occasions, disinterest in your personal life, moods or whatever else it is that happens in your house, all of these things are happening because the labels your teen uses to define who they are and how they 'fit in' are far more important than remembering Gran's birthday. It doesn't mean they love their Gran any less than they ever did. It's just that, in their world, there is something more important going on.

I'm not saying they are making good choices. What I am saying is that, if you cannot *accept* and *understand* this behaviour, you will reinforce their perception that they are 'right' and you'll be dancing the 'You Have No Idea What It's Like' Two Step again before you know it!

Of course this is an oversimplification – it's not always as clear cut. For some teenagers, even those with blue hair, a nose ring and that boy/girlfriend who you think is a really bad influence, 'family' may be a label they wear with immense pride and Gran's birthday will always be important.

But others just won't care.

You know your family better than anyone. But can you really honestly say that you know what labels are important to your teen?

I'm hoping that by now you'll be starting to look at your own situation and saying 'OK, *things need to change* . . .'

I wouldn't be surprised for that to be closely followed by, '*but how?*'

To answer that, let's revisit Buzz's story . . .

BREAKING THE RULES

When we left him, Buzz had just realised that everyone around him, especially Woody, had been telling him the truth all this time – he can't fly and his laser is a small red light. He accepts he is made of plastic and, the clincher, he has undeniable evidence that he is very, very breakable.

This new, vulnerable reality is a lot to deal with and he does what many people do when they realise that they are 'breakable' . . . he immediately gives up.

His courage, his resilience, his fearlessness and his positive attitude all disappear leaving Buzz a shell of his former self. How can he possibly continue when who and what he thought he was turns out to be almost 100% wrong?

In this instant, he is blind to his achievements, he disputes his many genuinely positive characteristics, he rejects all offers of kindness and friendship and that means he finds himself, very deliberately, alone.

All attempts to reach him fail.

In fact, he is so far gone that it appears he will let himself be completely destroyed rather than do anything to stop it. He seems unable to stand up, find his confidence and fight back.

At a point of crisis, Sid's collection of evil looking plastic hybrids who, up until this moment are assumed to be crazy, psycho toys, gather round Buzz in a mob. Buzz is sure that they are going to hurt him. Everyone watching, including us and Woody, are sure they are going to hurt him. But, in reality, it turns out they are there to help him.

They help him get himself together, pop his arm back in and stand him up, they show him empathy and understanding. In his moment of vulnerability, they help Buzz make two big changes.

1. He accepts that he is a toy.
2. He understands that being a toy doesn't stop him being every-thing he was before.

There are many times in life when all we need to know is that people are there for us, *especially* when it feels like everything we thought we knew has changed. Sometimes the person that is there for us is not who we expect, but that doesn't matter. It's just important to know that we have someone in our corner.

It's important to know we are not alone.

And, when we know we are not alone, we call it 'fitting in'.

As a parent you can often find yourself an outside observer. In order for that to change, you will need to accept that you are no longer the loudest and most important voice in your teenager's world.

Your teenager is at the beginning of a lifelong adventure during which they will create a world full of people who entirely understand their dances, thought processes and labels. And many of those other people will have voices that are louder and more influential than yours.

You cannot shout those voices down and you cannot fight them head on. To do that will only force you and your teen further apart. By this point in the book, you will know what you have to do instead.

Acceptance and understanding are the keys to change.

This does *not* mean that every teenage behaviour is acceptable! I am not in any way asking you to sit back and watch as your teenager cuts themselves, turns up drunk to school and screws their life up.

What I am saying is, the way to fit in to your teenager's world, in a way that ensures your voice has any volume, credibility or influence is to *accept* and *understand* their view of the world *before* you apply your own.

It's inevitable that as your teenager grows into themselves, they will make mistakes and you cannot prevent all these mistakes being made. And why would you want to? Learning from mistakes is vital to the process of growing.

What you can do is help prevent mistakes from having unnecessary, long term, negative effects. To understand this, let's close this chapter by taking a look at the basis of all our personality traits, the source of all our labels, the instruction book for who we are.

Let's look at our past.

The Magic of
Mistakes

SHADOWS OF OLD LEARNING

How did you end up being 'you'?

Think about who you are (or at least make your best guess) and think about how you ended up like this, having the lifestyle you have, doing the job you do, with the relationship you have (or don't have), with the friends you have (or don't have).

If you are not in a particularly introspective mood right now, then just focus on the last of those questions . . . think of your longest friendship(s) and ask yourself, why are you still friends?

I don't mean to plunge you into some sort of personal confidence crisis here! I'm really just looking for you to realise that, no matter what question you ask yourself, the answer will be broadly the same.

Experience.

You have *learned* to be here.

And that means you have *learned* to be you.

I'm going to ask you to put the book down and just consider that for a few minutes . . .

As you mature, your mind creates a vast library of everything that has ever happened, everywhere you have ever been, every person you have ever met and every experience you ever have ever had. It is all filed away in storage.

You know when you bump into someone and you recall their face from somewhere? You can't quite place them but it's obvious that they remember you perfectly. They know your kid's names, they know where you work, they even remember where you met, "Oh yes, of course we've met before. We spent hours drinking mojitos together at Charlie and Hilary's party about eight years ago. You must remember?"

For a brief moment the world stops as you think "Who the hell are Charlie and Hilary, when was their party and how did I make a complete fool of myself at that one?" Suddenly, as if from nowhere, your mind latches on to a memory and it all comes flooding back . . . "Of course we did, you were just back from your trip to Disneyworld that was a big surprise for your kids. Lovely to see you again Dave, how the devil are you . . .?"

The filing system in your brain has saved you and it's all flooding back to you now!

Unfortunately, in this particular case, it's *all* coming back and you pray that, while Dave may remember you, he won't remember your extravagant dancing to 'I Will Survive' and that unfortunate incident in the hot tub. In fact, you'd really rather *no-one* remembered that, even if it wasn't as bad as the thing your brother Andy did with the inflatable sheep at Jim and Emma's wedding . . .

This type of situation proves that the mind's library exists. The filing system isn't perfect, occasionally memories get fragmented and corrupted and mislaid, but they are all in there somewhere.

Funnily enough we didn't evolve this impressive ability solely to remember random people from parties eight years ago, even if that's pretty useful!

We actually evolved it to save us having to start from scratch every time we face something new. The library is where your mind finds the information it needs to help you make every decision you will ever need to make. If you are a parent, by this stage in your life, your library will be pretty well 'stocked'.

However, a teenager's library is a work in progress. Every decision they make can only be based on the life experiences they have collected up to this point.

They can't know what they have not experienced.

Let's look at a wee example to illustrate this . . .

Imagine a young child, playing innocently in the park, oblivious to the world around them as they roll down a small grassy hill and then run back to the top to do it all over again, giggling as they go.

In the midst of a particularly energetic roll, a big, fluffy, golden Labrador sees the fun and runs over to join in. As our little one gets to the bottom of the hill they are suddenly confronted by a huge dog standing over them, tongue out, teeth showing. The giggles are immediately replaced by a scream that can be heard from the other side of the park and then the tears begin.

The dog stands there wondering why the game has stopped!

For our little one, in that very instant, a memory has been created. It's already a really big memory with a ton of emotion packed into it and that means the mind will give it a very special, easily accessible space in the library.

The mind *needs* to remember this because it needs to keep us safe from that horrible thing ever happening again.

Fast forward to the next park visit. Unconsciously, our child's mind searches their library, finding every memory it has about the park and, wouldn't you know it, it remembers that big, scary memory from last time. Of course it would, their mind gave it a special place, front and centre, for this very reason and, because of what it remembers, it sounds a big alarm warning; 'this place is not safe!

As you get out of the car, you have no real idea what has changed their mood. You look to salvage your day, reminding your now screaming toddler about all the fun they have on the swings, how they love to feed the birds, they might even get an ice cream on the way home and if they don't calm down, they won't get to play with their friends.[3]

But they are having none of it.

All the happy memories associated with the park are entirely eclipsed by the memory of the snarling death beast that pinned them to the grass after they rolled down that hill.

As outside observers, we know that the dog meant no harm and just wanted to play. Because of our greater experience and our different perspective, we can see what happened in the proper context.

The toddler doesn't have the experience to interpret the situation and balance their innate fear response. And what we think we know doesn't matter because, again, *it's not about us.*

Unchecked, this scenario could be the beginnings of a lifelong fear of dogs and may be the last time this child ever experiences the joy of rolling down a hill without a care in the world. Their memory library has processed this experience as;

Park = DANGER!
Rolling down hills = scary animals at the bottom
Dogs = savage death beasts

And yet, that day at the park could have been so different . . .

---

[3] Um, pleasure and pain . . . just saying.

Imagine the dog hadn't been there. What would have been logged in the memory library instead was a great day out at the park rolling down hills.

Park = awesome place
Rolling down hills = awesome fun

Or imagine our wee person gets to the bottom of the hill, notices the big fluffy dog standing to the side secure on a lead looking over with its tail wagging. They run towards each other to say hello, the dog greets them with a huge face-lick and they run about playing with each other for ages.

Park = awesome place
Rolling down hills = awesome fun
Dogs = cuddly friends

This child loves the park, can't wait to roll down hills again and is a lifelong dog lover.

Our lives are made in moments.

All of those moments together make us who we are.

Charles Dickens puts it beautifully,

"Pause you who read this, and think for a moment of the long chain of iron or gold, of thorns or flowers, that would never have bound you, but for the formation of the first link on one memorable day."[4]

What memorable days are your children having right now?

---

[4] Dickens, C. *Great Expectations*. London: Penguin, 1996.

MADE OF MISTAKES

As teenagers, our kids are making their first huge decisions, shouldering adult responsibilities for the first time, and the only experiences they have to base these decisions on are from their childhood.

In essence, they are trying to make adult decisions with the resources of children and, when we appreciate this, we begin to understand that it's inevitable that they are going to get things wrong and this is no bad thing, no one learns anything when life is easy and everything goes our way.

Our ability to make good decisions comes from experience.

Experience tends to come from mistakes.

So, in simple visual terms,

Mistakes ↔ Experience ↔ Good decisions

Imagine a child who never makes a mistake at all through their early life. They are protected and shielded from all potential harm. Every decision they make works out and their parents work tirelessly to ensure that no action their child takes, or decision their child makes, ever goes wrong.

If they want it, they get it. If they break it, it's replaced. If something hurts them, it's immediately removed or fixed to ensure it will never hurt them again. If a friend is rude to them, they never play with that friend again. If they are rude, cheeky or naughty to anyone, they are never scolded.

Be honest, what kind of teenager do you think this child would become?

And can you imagine what will happen when this child turns up at high school, university or a workplace for the first time?

When our kids are young, it's easy for us to accept a broken toy, a grazed knee, a cheeky comment or a childhood falling out but, for some reason, once our child reaches the grand old age of teenager, any mistakes are frowned upon.

Why, all of a sudden, do we think they should 'know better'?

Your teen may no longer be learning how to run, how to climb a tree, how to ride a bike or how to get along with others in the play-ground, but that doesn't mean they aren't still learning about life.

For example, at some point in their teenage years, they will learn how romantic relationships work. They've never had one of these relationships before and that means they are going to make mistakes, mess up and of course, they are going to be over dramatic about the whole thing!

And this is where, if you are honest, some responsibility lies with you.

Ask yourself, as a parent, what lessons have you been teaching your kids about romantic relationships both in the past and right now?

If you think back to the 'library of memories', most of what teenagers know about relationships, at this stage of their lives, they will have learned from watching how their parent's relation-ship(s) work.

What is their experience of how to define a 'relationship'? Have you taught them well? When they go into their library and ask about romance what will they find?

Relationships = ?

Here's another . . .

This is the first time your teenager has ever been in a situation where they have to make choices and decisions as they learn what it means to be responsible for their own future.

What have you been teaching them, and what are you teaching them right now, about responsibility?

Most of what they know about being 'responsible' they will have learned by watching how you and the other key adults in their lives respond to work, pressure and adult responsibilities.

One more example . . .

Your teenager is learning how to be part of an adult social group for the first time. This is the first time they have ever been in situations where they are alone (i.e. without adult supervision) with alcohol, drugs, friendship and sex.

So what lessons have you been teaching them about alcohol, drugs, friendship, sex and being part of a functioning adult social group? Most of what they have learned about being social, they will have learned by watching how the adults in their life behave and 'fit in' socially. Do they need to be drunk to have fun? Do social groups have lots of people in them or just a few?

What have they learned from watching you?

Relationships = ?
Responsibility = ?
Social skills = ?

I know that in all three of these areas you will be teaching some amazing, valuable and enriching lessons. Lessons that will give your teen all the tools he or she needs to know exactly how to function and behave.

But we are all human. And that makes us fallible. We aren't perfect.

And therefore,

something you do is going to mess your kid up.

Yet at the same time,

every mistake is a chance to learn.

And this is true for both you and your teenager.

We will return to this in the next chapter. For now, please have a wee think about these two questions:

1. What are your actions teaching your teenager right now?

and

2. What are the experiences that they will use as references when they think of what you have taught them?

If you want to help your teenager grow and become a fully functioning adult, you need to help them. You need to *teach* them.

Sometimes you need to get angry and read them the Riot Act. Sometimes you need to sit still, stay calm and listen. Sometimes you will have to be a coach, pointing out consequences and outcomes to try and prevent disaster. Sometimes you just have to leave them to it and watch as they make a total mess of the whole thing.

A lot of the time you won't know what to do at all.

And that's OK.

Because if we are completely honest, we're all making it up as we go along. In most cases we don't know what we are going to do until we are doing it!

And that's how Buzz becomes more than just a toy.

WE CAN BE HEROES

Buzz and Woody are about to break *all* the rules.

It's the only way to get back to where they belong. It's the only choice left and, to get back to Andy, it's entirely worth it.

If you've never seen the movie (where have you been?), I won't ruin it by telling you exactly what they do or how they break the rules, but [spoiler alert!][5] the gamble pays off.

Buzz and Woody get back to where they belong but not before Buzz becomes a *real* hero. He is no longer someone plastered with false labels, pretending to be a hero. He steps up and shows that he is the real deal.

Now he has fully accepted his inability to fly, he saves the day by falling. With style.

Buzz Lightyear was never really an arsehole.

He was a hero in waiting, a hero who didn't realise why he was special. He thought his costume made him someone special, when actually he was special for who he was.

He had to learn how to be himself.

He had to learn to be a hero.

Just like you.

---

[5] Is it really a spoiler to say that a Disney/Pixar movie has a happy ending?

THE HERO'S SECRET

Have you ever parented your current teenager before?

Is this teenager exactly the same as any another teenager you have parented previously?

Did someone come along and offer you a practice run on being the perfect parent?

Do you have some sort of manual that shows you what to do when everything goes pear shaped?

I'll answer those questions for you right now.

No.

No.

No.

And . . . No!

You have no experiences on which to base your current parenting decisions for this particular teen and that means *you* are learning too. That's why you bought this book. You want to learn to be better. That's great, just remember this phrase for both you and your teenager . . .

Doing the best you can is the best that you can do.

But what we now know is that, in all the situations they end up in, at the root of all the behaviours our teens exhibit, there are two burning questions they are trying to answer; The Two Teen Questions.

"Who am I?" and **"How do I fit in?"**

And we also know, no matter what you have taught them, good or bad, right or wrong, virtue or anarchy, the answers to those questions will be found by one of three methods.

1. They will agree with you as a parent and embrace all you have taught them.
2. They will decide that your ways are rubbish and rebel.
3. They will do both!

Whichever they choose and, to be honest number 3 is most likely, it will lead to mistakes. They *will* regret choices and decisions they make, and they *will* do things you don't want them to do. Sometimes they will be right and it will work out. Other times, you may need to pick up the pieces. Just as you always have.

This whole chapter has been about helping you realise what an incredible and challenging task it is for any teenager to create an identity for themselves. This is especially true if they chose, consciously or otherwise, to ditch everything they knew before and start from scratch.

Your teenager is in the most intense period of emotional change they will ever experience and, even if it doesn't feel like it sometimes, you have a *vital* role to play.

If you are not prepared or are unable to accept what's going on, you will find yourself shut out, without influence, your role reduced to that of an outsider. If your teen can't 'fit in' at home they *will* go somewhere else.

Here's what to do . . .

Think before you speak.

It's important to ask yourself what you want your teenager to feel when you speak. If you want them to understand that you will support them to every success you believe they are capable of, is what you are about to say and, more importantly, *how* you are about to say it going to convey that?

Be mindful of your own state – if you are calm and understanding, the response you will get will likely be very different from what you will get if you are hysterical and angry.

Listen before you judge.

Remember, you are a parent of a teenager and you are no longer a teenager yourself. See the world through their eyes before you decide whether something is right or wrong. Could it just be different? This is not *your* life they're living, it's *theirs*.

Mistakes are inevitable – don't be surprised when they happen.

Embrace mistakes and find ways to ensure that positive lessons are learned from them, even if it's painful. This is how your teen will gain experience.

Don't rush in to pick up the pieces every time something goes wrong. Pain is a good, if harsh, teacher – try to judge when the repercussions of the experience have had sufficient time for the memories to be stored in the library before you do what you do to make it all better.

It's OK to want to rebel and try out new things.

Some of the most loving, caring and intensely special romantic relationships happen because a teenager watched mum and dad in a loveless/stormy/violent relationship and they rebelled *towards* love.

I know many people who don't drink alcohol because they watched alcohol ruin a life and they rebelled *into* sobriety.

It's quite common to find people who are hugely responsible, driven and ambitious because they grew up in an environment where none of those things were present and they rebelled *into* success.

Sometimes we rebel to save ourselves, not ruin ourselves.

But through every rebellious moment, mistake, judgment, angry word, door slam, you must *never* stop being a parent. Your job isn't finished, it has just become different.

Although they may tell you otherwise, in many situations you *do* know better because you have the experience they need for guidance. You are, and will be for many years to come, their most important teacher.

You just need to make sure you are a teacher that is heard and not a teacher who is ignored.

If you can understand all that, you're on the inside and starting to crack the Teen Code.

And now you're there, what the hell do you do now?

Funnily enough, we're just getting to that.

Chapter 3 – What The . . . ?

- Your teenager is the result of life-long programming, much of it performed entirely unwittingly by you, their parents! They are who you have made them.

- Identity is the key personality driver for a teenager. They will be telling you who they are by how they look and behave.

- If your teen doesn't feel like they fit in at home, they will find somewhere else to do it. You may not like where that somewhere else is.

- Acceptance & understanding are the keys to change. When someone accepts and understands, we know we are not alone.

- Every time the mind needs to make a decision, it first looks for experiences in the library of memories it has stored all of our life. What have you contributed to your teenager's library?

- Buzz Lightyear is a hero . . . and you can be too.

4

Yeah, No, Definitely, Maybe

Think about something you've been putting off for ages, some silly little task that needs doing but hasn't been done. Make it one of those things that you've said 'I'll get to that later' so many times that 'later' now means never!

Got a good example?

This little exercise takes a bit of focus so don't read on until you have time to do it properly.

Ready?

I want you, right now, this very second, to decide on a specific day, within the next week, when that task will be done.

Go for it! Make a decision right now.

Now, listen to what your internal voice is saying to you. I would guess that one of three things are happening . . .

1. You are coming up with excuses as to why this week isn't really a good time to do it. I mean, you have your mum's birthday and you haven't even got her a present yet and the kids have all those clubs during the week so there really isn't a good time for you to possibly fit it in. Even if you could, no-one else seems to care that you haven't done it yet so why bother putting yourself out? It would be much better to think about doing it

next week. Yep, definitely next week. Oh, but remember you have to go to that place to do that thing next week so that's probably not going to be good either. You can have another think about it later. There's no real rush is there?

Or . . .

2. You are congratulating yourself for finally committing to a date and deciding this task will at long last be sorted. If you are, that's great. You now have a plan that will guarantee you an amazing sense of achievement, no matter how small it is.

Or . . .

3. You are telling yourself you're not reading this book to do stuff for yourself, this isn't about you and you're not going to let a book force you to do things you don't want to do. Only *you* decide when you do things so you're just going to ignore it and keep reading. You'll do it when you are ready and not before.

Whatever you noticed during this wee exercise, there are two key points to remember:

You are normal.

and

You'll feel really good if you just do the damn thing already!

THE TECHNOLOGY OF DECISIONS

Your mind is a decision making machine. Every minute of every day we are making decisions, often without even realising it!

Before we are even properly awake, we make decisions about whether to snooze the alarm or just get up. We decide what clothes to wear. We decide what to have for breakfast. We decide if we are going to go to the gym now, later or just skip it again. In fact, I estimate that on a normal morning the average person probably makes 25 decisions before fully waking up.

And we don't stop decision making until we go to asleep again that night.

We are, in every sense of the word, a machine driven by our patterns and dances. These well practiced routines automate the majority of our day to day decisions, almost like an 'auto-pilot' that works away in the background to keep us ticking over with only minimal actual input required.

Think about that task you were putting off, I would bet that ignoring that task had become a habit. That is before you decided you were sorting it out this week of course!

Our patterns, habits, dances and routines allow us the space to make automated decisions so we can get on with the challenges that life throws at us on a daily basis. It is a highly efficient and effective way to work.

Imagine that I send a little brain fairy to your house (I have them you know!) with the mission of silently leaping into your head as you sleep and deleting all your patterned responses. This means that, when you wake up in the morning, every single thing you do will need to be decided from scratch.

EVERYTHING!

Do you snooze your alarm? Do you just get up? Do you shower before or after breakfast? Do you have a shower at all? Do you have breakfast? If you do neither what do you do instead? When you shower, do you wash your hair? Shampoo or shower gel? Do you have hair to wash? Do you spend hours in front of the mirror making yourself gorgeous? What does gorgeous even look like?

Do you like coffee? What do you take in your coffee? Maybe you should make 3 cups and experiment since you don't know what you like anymore.

What do you wear to work? When you finally choose, is it appropriate for where you work and what you do? How do you know? Should you call someone to check? Who would you call? How does your phone work? How would you find the number for the office? Should you Google it? What *is* Google?

Do you drive to work or get the bus? And does that dictate when you have to leave? How long does it take? Where is the best place to get the bus? Do you need cash or do you have a pass?

And I'm only just getting started here. Imagine how tired you would be by the time you got to work if this was your life. New decisions to be made about every single thing with no established patterns of behaviour or 'auto-pilot' responses to help.

Just imagine your mental state by the time you got back home again if every minute of your day presented you with something new that you had to learn to cope with, understand or manage.

It would be like being a teenager again!

Of course I'm exaggerating. I'm not suggesting that your teenager wakes up every morning and a brain fairy has deleted all their responses. You know that's not true because you'll recognise their established patterns and 'dances' on a daily basis.

However, in the course of their teenage years, teenagers find themselves in many, many situations for which they have no established patterns simply because, as we spoke about in the last chapter, they don't have the required experience.

Their brains will be frantically trying to establish a pattern but their 'machine' is being stretched to its limits. And with so much changing all the time, sometimes a pattern is still very very far away.

This is why your teen sleeps so much!! Their brain is knackered! But it is possible to make life easier when you understand the mechanics of decision making, why we often end up making ridiculous decisions and how to stop life being so damn confusing all the time.

MECHANICS OF THE MIND

Our brains use three techniques to make a decision: **Experience**, **Models** and **Dilemma**. These three techniques are fabulously efficient ways for our mind to navigate a complex world in ways that keep us safe and happy while using up as little energy as possible.

We've discussed how we use experience and models in previous chapters but let's look at them both in the context of decision making before we take a deeper look at dilemma-based decisions.

Mechanics of Mind: Experience

DÉJÀ YOU

Experience is absolutely, 100% the most reliable method we have for making any decision. It's the one we use for most of our everyday decisions because, simply put, life is so much easier when you've done it before!

Imagine how differently you would do things if you were told that everything up to now was a practice run and you were about to get another shot at life. I guarantee that, at the very least, some of your past fashion and hair style choices would be very, very different!

At its most basic and unconscious level, we are using our library of memories to do what we know works. If we have experienced it before, our mind will use that experience to tell us what to do next.

Of course, experience is also very useful if what you did before *didn't* work. In the instant of making a decision, our minds can just as easily recall the total mess we made of things the last time we did it and replays the whole disaster on a little screen inside our head. Our mind hopes we can use that experience to tell us what *not* to do and come up with a new approach. This new approach is not guaranteed to work but will, regardless, add to our accumulated experience and the process continues.

When we encounter a situation we haven't met before, our mind will check the library to see if it has information on it or, at least, anything a little bit similar. This is the basis of problem solving and abstract thinking – the ability to generalise previous experiences and apply them to something new. We can see one thing and realise that it could be something else, a stone could be an axe, a pond could be a mirror, a stick could be a fishing pole, a shell could be currency.

Nowadays, in this world of accessible technology, the same concepts can still apply. Have you ever been in a shop with a young child when they pick up an electronic gizmo they've never seen before and instantly know how to work it? It might not work exactly the same as the one they've used at home or at their friend's house or at school, but their mind accesses previous experience and previous learning then applies it to the similar situation.

However, this ability can also be the source of many of our problems.

In chapter 3, we discussed the scenario of a child 'learning' to be scared of dogs and we saw that they didn't develop a specific fear of big fluffy golden Labradors. They became scared of *all* dogs because the mind assumes that, if something is true of one thing, it must also be true of everything that is like that thing.

A teenager whose first relationship ends in heartbreak may find themselves reluctant to get involved in another in case the same thing happens again. Another teenager who finds that drinking alcohol helps them feel more confident can easily come to believe that the only way to be confident is to drink alcohol.

These 'mistakes' happen because, at this stage in our lives, we have no other experience on which to base our decisions. How can we be expected to make complex decisions about our future or respond appropriately to a new situation if we don't have anything in our library to explain what this new situation is?

What if our first relationship ends in heartbreak? Or we get bullied in our first job?

If it's our first time doing something and it gives us a negative experience, how do we know how to respond?

We may find some childhood memory in the library and try to apply it to the new situation but there's a very good chance that will end in disaster. Have you ever told your teenager that they should 'know better', that they're 'immature' or 'need to grow up'?

Have you ever considered that the behavior that led to those words happened because your teenager was applying childhood learning to the adult world, just as we saw in chapter 3? They are only building their library of experience. Remember, mistakes are inevitable.

The question is, what should your teenager do instead? If they don't have their own experiences to draw on, maybe someone else who *does* have experience can show them.

It's at this stage, they begin to *model*.

Mechanics of Mind:
Models

PARENTAL PLAGIARISM

Our library of memories contains vital information on all of the things we have seen other people do and how they have behaved. Even if we have no memories of other people doing what they do we are surrounded by people we can ask; teachers, parents, mentors, peers, family.

The mind, being a resourceful machine, can, in the absence of a specific personal experience, use this information, gained from other people, to generalise a response and apply it to our own world.

The best examples we have of this are the people we look up to. We even call them our *Role* Models, people we strive to be like by imitating and asking for advice. We look to apply their behavior to our world. We try to make decisions in the same way they do.

My two daughters are both uncomplaining studiers. When it comes to the pressure of exams, we rarely have to encourage them to start 'hitting the books'. Both are happy to retreat to a quiet room with their books, highlighters, sticky notes and paper to study for hours.

I know! You're wondering how the hell we got that lucky, aren't you? The question is, were they born this way or were they *programmed*?

Do you think it is a coincidence that, for six years of their young lives they saw their mum studying for hours on end? Before they even reached an age where exams were part of their lives they witnessed their mum proudly gain a First Class Honors Degree and achieve the dream opportunity to enter the career she always wanted. Could they have been influenced by this?

When exams came about, they looked to mum for advice, support and help. They had watched her do it so they knew that she had what they needed to succeed.

Unknown to them (and us) they had the perfect model at the perfect time. My kids thought study was 'normal' from an early age and the pattern was ingrained for them to use later.

In theory, it's pretty easy to be like your role models, to achieve the things they achieved and make the decisions they made.

However, because it's so easy, sometimes modeling turns out to be a negative.

How many teenagers have unconsciously modeled anxiety, depression, self harm, smoking, drinking, relationship problems, negative attitudes to life and a whole heap of other negative behaviours? In the absence of personal experience, the only logical way they could have learned how to do these things is if they witnessed them in their parents or other role models.

You cannot control every role model your child has and therefore there is no way to fully protect against them modelling a negative. But you can control the role model that *you* are.

With that in mind, I have a simple thought for you to consider.

Be the person you want your child to be.

Simple as that.

If you want to give your child the best chance of growing up a good person, *be a good person*.

If you want to give your child the best chance of growing up ambitious and confident, *be ambitious and confident*.

If you want to give your child the best chance of having a loving, caring and respectful relationship . . . realise your children are watching and you are, right now, teaching them what love is. Do you want them to have the relationship you have? I sincerely hope you do because that will mean you have a solid, loving and caring relationship.

Your teenager is currently making many of their decisions based on the behaviour of their models. They *need* to do this to build enough experiences of their own to make good decisions.

Although it might not feel like it sometimes, their number one models will be their parents.

Be the person you want your child to be.

You may have a lot more experience than your teen but you haven't experienced absolutely *everything*. This means there will be an inevitable situation when your teenager needs to make a decision, finds that they have none of their own experience to help and no appropriate models with the required experience either.

There will also be other situations when their experience and their models conflict.

It's because of this we that we need a third way of deciding what to do.

We call this *dilemma*.

Mechanics of Mind: Dilemma

POLES APART

When a parent calls me and asks me to help their teenager sort out their mind, one of the first questions I ask is "Is it like there are two Lauras?"[1] I'm trying to find out if it seems like there are two 'personalities' at play in the teenager's patterns of behaviour.

Often one 'personality' is the 'normal' teenager that the parent recognises and knows, while the other seems to be completely out of character – anxious, angry, depressed, lazy or any other emotion where the intensity is turned up to eleventy-stupid.

These two personalities will alternate in an instant, like someone is flicking a switch inside their brain.

A peaceful and pleasant family dinner can suddenly be interrupted by raised voices, swearing and the slamming of doors with no apparent reason for the sudden emotional explosion.

A fun shopping trip can be abruptly cut short as a huge anxiety attack appears out of nowhere. No amount of reasoning and calm talking is going to convince your teenager that anything less than getting home *right now* is the answer.

You can watch as a normally happy and confident young person suddenly disappears into themselves and becomes shy, withdrawn and distant. You try and remind them of how they 'usually are' but for some inexplicable reason they seem frustratingly (and thankfully only temporarily) stuck.

As a parent, these are the moments in which you feel most helpless.

---

[1] Obviously this question changes depending on the teenager's name – I don't ask *every* parent if there are two Lauras!

You know your 'normal' teenager is in there. You know it doesn't have to be like this. But you can't help. You can't seem to find a way 'in'.

At this point, I need to remind you that

acceptance and understanding are the keys to change.

And with that in mind, let's talk about marshmallows.

PATIENCE PAYS

There is a very famous psychological experiment called the Stanford Marshmallow Experiment[2] (yes, really!).

A young child is placed in a room and given some sort of individual sweet or a single desirable treat by an adult who gives them one simple instruction – if they can resist eating the treat until the adult comes back into the room, they will be given a second one and they can have both. Simple as that.

The adult then leaves the room for 5 minutes and watches the drama unfold.

Some children go right ahead and eat the treat as soon as the adult leaves. The experience they need to decide to leave it for the greater reward has not been established and therefore if you put a treat in front of them, they're just going to eat it![3]

---

[2] This experiment was also used in a recent UK TV advert for Haribo sweets. For more scientific info check out http://psychology.wikia.com/wiki/Stanford_marshmallow_experiment

[3] It is possible that there may be children who know from previous experience that one treat is enough for them. I have never met any such children.

Other children fully understand the concept. They already have enough experience to know that it is entirely worth the wait and the decision to sit back, relax and wait for the adult to return before enjoying double the treats is made almost instantly.

And then there are the children with a *dilemma*.

They have a full-on fight with themselves. They have just enough experience to tell themselves they should wait, but the childlike instinct to stick the treat in their mouths and enjoy it straight away is very, very powerful.

This is dilemma. Stuck between two decisions and not enough experience or a good enough model to help choose which one is best.

In the experiment, many do choose to succumb to temptation and then feel guilty or remorseful when the adult comes back into the room. Even at this young age they understand what they *'should'* have done, but didn't.

This is also a common result of dilemma. Choosing the path of least resistance, the one that takes least energy, and then regretting the decision.

At the age of the children in this experiment, typically 4–6, these experiences are just simple little dilemmas that rarely cause any long term effects. However, if we upgrade the concept to a teenager-sized dilemma, it's a very different story.

Imagine the 'treat' is now a school trip, let's say a week away somewhere exciting and outdoorsy.

Going on this trip will give your teenager incredible experiences, a chance to bond with their classmates and other people their own age from other places around the country. It is the promise of an adventure and the opportunity to do a whole heap of things they wouldn't normally get the chance to do. It will be an amazing week that they will look back on as a fantastic experience.

That all sounds exciting doesn't it? Well it does to us as parents, with our years of experience and the gift of hindsight.

But your teenager doesn't have that. They are in conflict and an internal, unseen fight is beginning.

They know all the good things that *could* come from this experience but, at the same time, there is another part of their mind telling them about all the bad things that *could* come from this experience.

Could. In a dilemma, this is a very powerful word.

Your teenager asks themselves, 'How do my parents know what *will* happen? They don't know what *will* happen, they must mean what *could* happen because they can't really be sure. Or can they? How's that possible?'

Without any experience to call on, your teenager can easily end up as stuck as the children in the marshmallow experiment. Their mind follows exactly the same process.

They don't know what to do. They have promises of good stuff that's going to happen but there is also a huge unknown where any number of bad things could happen too. There is no definite.

There is only dilemma.

Just a brief aside . . . imagine how this would change if they go on the school trip and have a fantastic time. When the offer comes to do it again, do you think there will be the same dilemma? As long as the variables stay the same or at least broadly similar, they'll be at the front of the queue to sign up.

This concept is really important to understand, because teenage life is one great big mixing pot of dilemmas.

There are many common patterns of dilemma that almost all teenagers will pass through at some point. For example;

• **Friendship Dilemmas:** long held close friendships can fall apart as 'fitting in' dilemmas surface. For example, 'am I good enough?' and 'do people like me?' or even 'am I a horrible person?'

• **Sexuality Dilemmas:** a dilemma that can be simply summarised in one question; 'do I like girls or boys?' The answer to this one is often much more obvious than it seems, however previous 'am I good enough?' and larger fitting in dilemmas can get in the way and complicate matters.

• **Passion and Interest Dilemmas:** Sometimes sports, fitness, dancing or musical interests, which have been a huge part of their lives up to now, suddenly lose their appeal. They want to but, at the same time, they don't. All feelings of fun and enjoyment disappear and the whole thing becomes a trial and in many cases, it isn't long before they just give up.

But to really explain how to help our teens climb out of this situation, let's look at one of the biggest problems our teens face today which is almost entirely caused by dilemma. Let's look at anxiety.

Anxiety:
the 'What If?' Problem

DOCTOR, DOCTOR, GIMME THE NEWS

Before we get into the dilemma of anxiety, let's just make one thing really clear. If your child has an emotional problem you need to know that your teenager is NOT broken, they are NOT unwell, they do NOT have a disease and they can, and most likely will, be OK if someone can simply explain what's going on in a way they can understand and relate to.

However, before that happens, many parents will go and do what is 'normal'. They will go to their doctor.

If you take your teenager to the doctor and explain a set of symptoms including any combination of phobias, extreme emotional reactions, excessive use of drugs and/or alcohol, self harm, eating disorders, body image disorders, poor memory, chronic fatigue, panic attacks and/or isolation from their peer group (these are just a few examples off the top of my head) there is a strong possibility you will be offered medication.

Sometimes this is absolutely the right course of action to take. The right medication at the right time can help steady the ship, calm things down and allow everyone some space to gain perspective and work out a positive way forward.

However, in my opinion, what medication is not, and never will be, is a *solution*.

It's a *crutch*.

If you break your ankle you would obviously go and get medical attention as quickly as possible. I'm pretty sure you would be more than a little annoyed if the doctor gave you no pain killing medication, no x-ray on the bone, no cast to hold it steady and simply told you not to worry, it will all be fine, just keep going, be careful when you walk on it but they are pretty sure it will fix itself in time.

Of course this would never happen. They would reset the bone, fix it firmly in place with a plaster cast, give you suitably powerful pain killers to ensure a level of comfort and give you a crutch to keep the weight off it as the body begins the healing process. In time you would be sent for a lengthy course of physiotherapy to get all the muscles, tendons, ligaments and bones strong again, ensuring no lasting damage.

Let me share with you what happens to many people when they feel they are not doing well emotionally. For some reason, their mind isn't doing what they want it to and something just didn't feel right, so they go to the doctor.

The doc is sympathetic and says that they know exactly what's wrong, which is of course a huge relief. In all the stories I hear from my clients, at this point, three things happen . . .

1. The doctor diagnoses that they are 'broken' in some way.
2. They give a prescription for a tablet to 'take the weight off', to 'stop things getting to you' and generally 'lighten your emotional load'.
3. They explain that the tablets will have to be taken long term, possibly forever, because that's the only way they could 'cure' the problem.

Compare this to our physical ailment – the broken ankle. When do we reset the mind and get it all nice and straight again? What do we use to hold it all in place while we make it strong again? Where is the physiotherapy? Why are you given a crutch to take the weight off and told it's a cure? Why do you have to take it forever? Surely the actual definition of a 'cure' is something you *don't* have to take forever?

This approach isn't really helping. This is just covering the problem up and, I promise, if you don't listen to your mind and feelings, it will come back and it will come back worse than before. Your body and mind will demand that you pay attention to them when they are telling you that something's out of balance by giving you symptoms. Drugging your emotions might calm things down in the short term but, over time, your mind will find a way to resist, fight back and turn up the volume until you have no choice but to listen.

Your mind will be heard. Even if it has to scream.

That is why it is so important for us to help ourselves and our teens when our minds stop doing things the way we expect them to. We need to listen.

We need to know how to administer emotional first aid.

THE CURSE OF THE "WHAT IFS"

When you look at it carefully, anxiety is actually very, very simple. An ankle is way more complicated with all its bones, muscles and all the other stretchy and jointy bits (I was never very good at biology).

All anxiety, and most teenage drama is caused by one big question.

'What if . . .?'

By this point in the book, you'll be fast becoming an expert in the teenage mind. So I'm going to test you with a couple of 'What If' scenarios and ask you consider the dilemmas that could result.

Scenario 1

A teenager is invited on a week long school trip to an outdoor centre (a familiar one to get started).

Their parents tell them about all the amazing things that will happen when they go away on the residential week. They'll abseil down a cliff, walk through a gorge, kayak on a loch and will have loads of fun.

What is the voice inside the teenager's head saying as they decide to go or not?

Is it,

(a) What if I make an idiot of myself and wet the bed/fall of a cliff/fall out of the kayak/get lost and everyone laughs at me?
(b) What if I'm fatter/skinnier/taller/shorter/spottier than everyone else and everyone finds out and laughs at me?
(c) What if I get homesick and start crying in the middle of the night because I want to go home and everyone laughs at me?
(d) What if I get left out and end up on my own because none of my friends are going and no-one there actually likes me and everyone laughs at me?
(e) What if all of the above happen?

Scenario 2

A teenager is sitting alone in their room. In their house. Safe from harm.

What is the wee voice inside the teenager's head screaming?

(a) No-one likes me. They only pretend.
(b) I'm disgusting and nowhere near as pretty/handsome as other folk in school.

(c) I am far too stupid to get the grades I need.
(d) Everyone in school thinks I'm weird and strange and I have no friends.
(e) What if it's all true?

How did you get on?

To be honest, this wasn't the hardest test ever as there really are no wrong answers! Whatever you said, you're right. *All* of these are genuine statements that teenagers hear inside their head. And *all* of these cause teenagers anxiety.

However, it is important to know that, in *every* case, there is another wee voice, often much quieter, and it's fighting back. This wee voice tries to pick out positive experiences to balance the negative ones.

But their mind does not have the experience to give this wee voice any credibility. Pain is, as always, the most powerful motivator. We fear pain far more than we crave pleasure.

This is the dilemma of anxiety. In this example, one side sees the pain and wants to protect while the other sees the pleasure and wants to experience.

You are now seeing why teenagers act in ways that take them further away from what they actually want.

Imagine the internal thought process of anxiety. Look for the dilemma between the two 'voices', remember one will be much quieter than the other;

> "What if I am weird and no-one likes me? I saw a thing online that said cutting can make you feel better. Everyone is doing it. Well, everyone who thinks they are a weirdo like me is doing it. And I'm like them. I could try it. People are even posting pictures of their cuts online. Why not, I'm weird anyway? Just once. Why not join this online group and give it a go . . .?"

"Wow! What a rush! It kinda hurt and left a bit of a mark but now I fit in with these people. This is amazing . . . I'll remember this next time I need to make a decision about how to feel better."

"But now the rush is fading, I feel guilty and ashamed about what I've done. The cuts on my arm are really bad and I'll be too embarrassed to go swimming when we go on holiday next week. I was really looking forward to that too. Mum and Dad will go crazy. Didn't think about that. I'm such a failure."

"I don't know how, but Mum saw my cuts. She went mad and started shouting and screaming and crying. She scared me and I felt bad but she doesn't know what it's like to be me. She said she was ashamed of me . . . yeah, well that makes two of us. Dad will probably agree with her. He already thinks I'm weird because I don't have any friends. I wish I had friends. But most people agree with Dad and think I'm a bit weird."

"I just feel crap. I don't fit in anywhere but I wish I did. Other kids seem to find it all so easy. Why don't I? Well, I suppose I fit in online. They get it. They know what it's like to be me, to be weird. They are my friends. I remember that rush from last time and I know I'll feel better if I do it one more time, but just once more. This'll be the last time though. I don't want Mum to shout at me again but yeah, just this one last time . . ."

I'll leave you to substitute the self harm in the above example with smoking, parties, drinking, purging, sex, or any other behaviour linked to extreme anxiety. It's easy to see how the teenage mind finds it easy to get trapped.

With this context, it's easy to see why medication is not a cure. No pill is going to make a 16 year old feel accepted. It will just numb the feelings that come from being confused.

In this face of these issues, we must ensure our parental approach remains based on the acceptance and understanding we discussed earlier. Even when you are scared, even when you are worried, even when you don't know what else to do and all seems lost, dark or the worst it could ever be.

When we shout at it, when we force our way on to someone that doesn't want our way, we compound it and we will very quickly become part of the problem.

Remember,

every pattern of behaviour exists for a positive reason.

Every pattern of behaviour.

Look at the cutting example I gave above. That teen's mind isn't trying to scar them or cause them unnecessary pain. There are two obvious positive outcomes from our example above; emotional release and finding somewhere they fit in.

In avoiding the school trip our teenager is staying safe and protected from potential danger. The fact that the danger is entirely imagined is of no relevance to the thought process. Their mind is trying to achieve safety and protection, and staying home is the easiest route. Experience tells us that we are safe in the house, going on the trip is too full of uncertainty.

Have you ever run away screaming from a small, completely stationery spider on a wall of your house?

Imagine in that moment, I started shouting that the danger you are experiencing was not real and there was absolutely no reason for your response. Would you just stop, realise I was totally right and immediately feel fine, making friends with your new spider buddy and letting them crawl over your hand?

If you're honest, you know you would still end up on top of the washing machine screaming for someone to get the horrible thing out of the house.

In moments of dilemma, we will listen to and act upon our emotions before we listen to reason.

When we're trying to 'fix' or 'get rid of' a side of our teenager's mind that is there to protect them and keep them safe from danger we lose our connection and empathy.

Your teen will feel that.

We don't need to fix or get rid of anything. We are focusing far too much on *what* is happening and nowhere near enough time thinking about *why* it is happening.

**The things we do are not *who we are*,
they are just things we do.**

We need to understand that both sides of any dilemma are trying to help.

We need to spend less time discussing 'right' and 'wrong'.

We need to stop medicating our kids to make them be quiet and behave as we think they should behave.

We need to stop trying to fix things that aren't actually broken.

We need to change what our teens do by accepting and under-standing *why* they do it.

We need to find balance.

THE PARTY STOPS

The key to stopping a dilemma permanently is all about helping their minds to find a place where they can achieve *both* positive outcomes.

Protected *and* fun.

Calm *and* fitting in.

Safe *and* confident.

There are two important factors to remember here:

1. **Change happens in seconds but it can take time for those seconds to happen.**
   It takes time because the person changing has to be willing and ready to change. And they won't be ready to change until they know, absolutely *know*, that when they change they are still going to be safe, loved and protected.

2. **The positive reason may be hidden from them as well as you.**
   Why do we do the things we do? At the moment we start doing them the deep psychological need that they meet is often hidden from us. Especially as that 'thing' becomes normal. How many of us would recognise a deep reason for our morning cup of coffee? It exists, but would you know what it is if I asked you?

The only person that can ever know the positive reason for a negative behaviour is the person actually doing it. When it is your teenager, your job is to help them find it and guide them to a better way.

Let me explain the hidden secret of every dilemma.

When any event occurs, the mind instantly decides the positive outcome it wants to achieve e.g. happiness, love, confidence, peace, connection, safety, control or whatever. From that moment, every decision we make, and action we take, is based on finding the shortest route from where you are now to that positive outcome.

The secret of a dilemma is simply;

Both sides of any internal dilemma are aiming to achieve the same positive outcome.

In a given situation, the wee voice telling us we should do something is looking to achieve exactly the same positive outcome as the wee voice telling us we shouldn't. The problem is that the behaviours our 'voices' are choosing between are complete opposites!

In our examples we have a teenager that wants to go on school trip to be liked and appreciated but can't go on the trip in case they aren't liked or appreciated. One voice wants to achieve it through interaction and communication and the other wants to avoid not achieving it by staying home, safe and alone.

The teenager who cuts themselves because they have bottled up all their problems and emotions until they are overwhelmed, just wants to be left alone in their misery. At the same time they desperately want to be heard but, because they have bottled up all their problems and emotions, they don't know how to seek help or speak about the issues.

One voice wants to achieve peace and emotional release in solitude and safety while the other voice urges them to achieve peace and emotional release through connection and honesty.

The teenager having an anxiety attack about going to school while crying about how they are messing up their whole future by not going to school, is worried about both going and not going.

One voice is urging them to run away and hide to be calm, secure and happy, while the other is urging them to run towards, embrace school and learning and all the good things it will bring them so they can be calm, secure and happy.

Does that make sense?

In all those examples both sides want the same result but they have entirely opposite ways to achieve it.

Helping someone solve a dilemma is about allowing them the space to explore what is actually going on, guiding them to the insight that the negative behaviour is only one choice of ways to achieve what they want.

Let the behaviour show itself, accept it for what it is, ask questions to understand why it's happening and realise that you are not going to change anything by fighting it. Remind yourself that what is happening to your teenager is really scary for them too and is not what either of you want. As you accept and understand what is going on and foster the same in your teenager, you will begin a process of change.

The moment your teen understands that anxiety does not mean they are broken and is, in fact, one of the mind's protection mechanisms. The moment they understand that their short temper does not mean they are a bad person; it is merely the mind looking to be heard and defend itself against a perceived attack. The moment they realise their mind has chosen a negative behaviour because it is the quickest way to achieve a positive outcome, the moment they realise that other more positive behaviours will work just as well.

In these moments, change begins.

In all these cases, you are in the perfect position to enquire if the mind is protecting or defending. And by finding out what it is protecting or defending against, everyone can begin to understand and accept what is really going on.

The better you can understand what is going on, the more chance you have of successfully guiding your teenager through the minefield of hormones, changes, emotions and finding who they want to be.

To finish this chapter, let's lay out the roadmap for teenage change and what to do when you inevitably meet resistance against your efforts to help.

The Stages of Change

DO YOU WANT TO PLAY A GAME?

When helping a teenager change, you must remember that they will use some very rudimentary defence tactics. As you get close to any emotional 'stuff', especially if they are trying to keep it hidden, they will feel vulnerable and struggle with strong emotions of fear. They will react first and think later.

In reality, there are five stages of change, the first four of which are actually reactions to the *fear* of change.

Just think about that for a minute.

In my experience, there are four possible reactions to fear that do not necessarily proceed in a linear manner but can be used as a guide to show which stage you and your teenager are at within the process of making changes.

It is possible to jump from one stage to any other in an instant with the right (or indeed wrong) words, action or approach. It is always our aim in any process of change to make the quickest jump to stage 5.

Stage 1 – Freeze (apathy)

A common teenage mindset this one. "I don't care", "I'm not bothered", "Do what you want", "Whatever" or some other verbal/physical indicator of an emotional void.

It's nice and safe in an emotional void. You can pretend that you don't care and never show anyone that you actually *do* care deeply but are simply afraid you'll get hurt. In the void, you are protected in case something bad happens and if you disengage completely, you don't have to *feel*.

To be honest with you, I spent a lot of my teenage years in this place! "Brian's so laid back he could be backwards". Actually, I was just keeping myself safe in a place where I outwardly appeared as if I cared about nothing.

Dealing with apathy is difficult because it is nothing.

There is no up, no down, just *nothing*.

So what do you do? Well, this may seem extreme but I call it 'poking with a stick'! If they want to pretend they don't care enough to react, keep on at them until they do. You are about to become the most annoying parent in the world!

"How was school today then?"
"Fine."
"Sounds good, what was fine about it?"

"Are you ready for your exams?"
"Yeah, maybe. I think so."
"Excellent, show me what you've been doing."

You need to be a little bit in their face, gently and persistently. They have learned that if they shut you out, they can shut the fear out, You have to prove to them that it is OK to let you in.

This doesn't mean the emotional door will suddenly be thrown open for you but, at the very least, you will provoke some sort of response. And it's somewhat likely that response will be . . .

Stage 2 – Fight (anger)

This is the most powerful defensive reaction your teenager has to fear. Especially if they perceive you to be the source of their fear.

A shout, a scream, "leave me alone", "you have no idea what you are talking about", "if you don't stop, I will <insert crazy behaviour here>".

This is a defence entirely designed to get you to back off by causing you *pain*. Stage 2 includes guilt trips, physical threats, emotional blackmail and anything else they can think of to get you to leave them alone.

Looking at it in a more positive way, you can tell you have touched a nerve! This kind of reaction is better than no reaction at all. There is a common mistake that parents make here which is to match the anger and get angry back.

That gets us nowhere.

In fact, it simply creates more fear and will likely reinforce their fear that you don't know what they are going through.

Instead, the way forward is again acceptance and understanding and to recognise that the anger is a way 'in'.

Remember the process we discussed earlier,

Trigger > Thought > Feeling > Action

Your teen is currently *feeling* and it's your job to figure out the *thought* that caused it.

What are they defending against? Why is that anger showing up now?

Think like a detective, the clues will be there. Remember they are angry because they are scared. If you approach this with acceptance and understanding, you will help them realise that they are safe.

If you shout back, you will simply push them into Stage 3.

Stage 3 – Flight (escape)

The easiest way to escape from fear? Run away!

"I don't need to listen to this", "I'm not talking to you anymore", door slamming, a hastily grabbed jacket and a front door left swinging on its hinges in their wake.

The more vulnerable your teenager feels, the more their mind looks to regain control. By far the easiest way is to just escape, get out, get far away from whatever is causing these feelings.

They don't need to go far to escape, just somewhere that's not here.

Although you do of course need to keep everyone safe, remember this is simply a sign that an emotional nerve has been touched. The question bubbling away in your head should be "what are they so scared of?"

If you can, don't let them escape. Follow them. Open the door, go into the room, engage them. Don't let them run away from the problem but at all times we are approaching this from a place of care, love, acceptance and understanding.

If you don't do this and barge in, shouting, screaming and telling them how bad everything is then you will just reinforce the fear. You will bounce between Stages 2 and 3 forever.

However, if you are patient, if you can show them that you really do want to help, if you can allow them to perceive you as safe, you will guide them towards Stage 4.

Stage 4 – Fold (vulnerability)

"I don't mean it, I don't mean to shout and get angry".

Here we go. Nearly there. Whatever you're doing is working.

Emotional vulnerability means that Trust has been gained. This is hugely positive but you cannot stop pushing. We are not there yet.

I know it's your little baby and of course you want to cuddle them and make sure they are OK but while you do that, keep the conversation going and keep *listening*.

At stage 4, the information tends to be unfiltered and raw. What is said at this point will reflect their true, innermost thoughts and you need to listen to the *meaning* of the stories, rather than the content.

It doesn't matter if they give you ten minutes on all the friendship drama that has been happening if you miss the point where they say "but nobody likes me anyway".

In this state of acceptance and vulnerability, your teenager is emotionally exposed. It is vitally important that you realise that, at this stage, they will allow you to be their model and guide.

My advice at stage 4 is to stay calm. You may hear things that you don't expect. You may hear things that scare you, worry you or upset you but this is the time to use everything you have learned in this book.

Ask questions *before* giving advice.
Make sure your words match your intention.
Be a listener more than a talker.
Be a role model.
Show them love.

Ensure they know they are not alone.
Let them know you've got their back.

Once the lines of communication are open, work to keep them open and the emotions flowing. Empty out as much of the emotion as you can before you start putting everything back together.

At this point, you are on the very edge of . . .

Stage 5 – Change

You've made it!

This stage can truly transform your teenager and your whole family dynamic.

Remember, when a person is ready for change, that change will happen in seconds. When someone feels safe, trusted, supported, loved, accepted and whatever else they need, change will be quick and easy.

But there is an important point to remember here. Family change is not a one-way street. If your teen is changing then you will have to change too.

If you say you are going to be more caring and understanding, do a weekly day out where you go for coffee and a trip to the cinema or if you promise to make family time a priority over work then you need to make sure *you* deliver.

If your teen learns that you don't keep your promises, what do you think will happen next time they need someone to talk to about their 'stuff'? Are they going to come to you when their experience tells them you let them down or are they going to choose someone else?

I know you love your teenager dearly. I know you think that every-thing you do for them proves they are loved and cared for. You don't pick them up from distant parties at 1am because you enjoy night driving. A powerful parental cocktail of worry, care and love gets you in the car because leaving them walking the streets at that time of night just isn't going to happen.

But to them, that's not really proof that you love them. It's just a lift home. It's normal.

If you moan at them about doing it, they may even perceive that they are causing you hassle and if you're making such a big fuss, clearly you don't care about them. Remember that your outward emotions and actions (being annoyed about having to pick them up) will mask your true intention (keeping them safe because you love them).

My advice – once you are changing, tread carefully and respectfully. The door can close just as quickly as it opened.

Change happens when there is acceptance and understanding.

Be accepting of any steps backwards. They will happen and you may have to start all over again. Being a teenager is strangely scary but if you can make acceptance and understanding part of your normal family dynamic, change and trust will be a constant part of your normal too.

PEACEFUL MOMENTS

As a parent, you are a part of a team of role models who are all training your teenager to make huge life-defining decisions. I hope that you are still a critical and significant part of that team but, if for some reason you are not, then you must accept that and contribute what and where you can.

All is not lost. If you approach things in the right way, you can get back in.

Your teenager is no longer a small child who sees you as infallible. They are now becoming, and maybe already are, an adult. They can see your mistakes, they know you have vulnerabilities and they don't necessarily share all of your values. It is also true that, although you still see moments of immaturity, they don't. To them, they are, in their world, a fully-fledged and experienced adult.

You need to be aware that your old way of getting things done may not work anymore. You can no longer shout an instruction and use fear to get them to do what you want. If you shout, they will shout back!

The response you get on any given day depends on a hundred different factors ranging from exam stress to the last time they ate but whatever response you get, if your shouting was unwarranted, unexplained and perceived as unfair, then the path to acceptance and understanding, and therefore the door to change, has become a little harder to open.

You will have noticed that the theme of this chapter has been *balance*. To be a good parent you must ensure that you think about balance in every interaction. Sometimes shouting is required and sometimes quiet, caring words are required. What message is your teenager receiving from your behaviour and actions?

If I was to ask your teenager about where your behaviour sits on a scale of pleasure to pain, what would they say?

Think about it. Be honest.

As much as you can, try to ensure that every necessary pain is balanced with an appropriate pleasure, and give your teen as many experiences as you can to prove they are not broken, faulty or alone.

Every pattern of behaviour exists for a positive reason.

We have learned that acceptance and understanding of our teenagers' behaviours will reveal a true picture of what is going on. We have learned that we are decision making machines which arrive only semi-assembled and, although we have all the tools we need to put it together, we don't have any instructions or even a picture of what it should look like. Every step requires a bit of guesswork.

At least now we have learned what the mind's main functions are and how it can get itself all mixed up. It seems that having a screw loose isn't as bad as we might have thought – it only means that particular screw needs tightened to make everything run smoothly again.

Now all we need to do is figure out how to keep the machine moving in the right direction.

Chapter 4 – What The . . . ?

- There are three ways to make a decision – Experience, Models and Dilemma.

- Teenagers can often make mistakes when they apply childhood experience to the adult world. They don't know anything else. It's to be expected.

- Be the person you want your child to be. Be their first role model. If you can't be that then do not be surprised when they keep you locked out.

- Dilemma is at the root of almost all teenage emotional issues. The mind is stuck between two behaviours trying to achieve the same intention. Change will happen when the intention is revealed.

- There are four F'ing reactions to fear – Freeze (apathy), Fight (anger), Flight (escape) and Fold (vulnerability). Respond to what is happening, do not reflect it back. Being angry at them for being angry will only lead to stalemate.

- Acceptance and understanding are the keys to change. You do not have to agree or like the choices your teenager is making, but if you can understand it and accept that, at this moment in time they are making the best choices they are able to with their limited experience, you have far more chance of helping them.

5

Unstoppable Forces

There are a set of well known philosophical conundrums that have evolved through time to teach and encourage critical thinking. My favourite of these, known as the Shield and Spear Paradox, poses the question, 'What happens when an unstoppable force meets an immovable object?'

The paradox is obvious – at some point, in this theoretical coming together, something will *have* to give. Either the unstoppable force will be stopped or the immovable object will be moved. However, if and when it does at least one of the descriptions is shown to be false.

You may be under the impression that you have an immovable object in your house (aka a teenager). However, although they may appear to be immovable, I promise this perception is also false.

You *can* move them.

You just need to be the unstoppable force!

Let's be clear, being unstoppable does not mean charging head-long at your teenager with a barrage of inspiring quotes about 'being all you can be' and 'living the life of your dreams' hoping your teen buckles under the weight of your motivational flood, breaks down in tears (see previous chapter) and exclaims 'Hallelujah parents, my life is saved' before immediately hitting the books, studying to get into the best University and living the life you dreamed for them.

That's not an unstoppable force, that's a bloody nightmare!

In the same way, this isn't about refusing to listen to reason, deciding you know best and demanding your teenager follows a set of strict and rigid rules and procedures that will micro manage their life until they become a successful, happy and fulfilled adult.

I would hope by this point in the book you would see that the psychology of both these approaches are outdated and much more likely to lead to disaster than any level of happiness.

So how *do* we do it? How do we get our, apparently, immovable object to move?

Well first we need to understand that we can't actually move it at all. We can only suggest it moves itself.

We call this *motivation*.

KEYING THE CODE

Think about something you really love to do. Something that, if you had the chance to do right now, you would be up and ready in no time at all.

Now think of the three biggest reasons why you love to do that thing.

Were any of the reasons you just thought of 'motivation'?

OK, let's try again.

Just like we did at the beginning of the last chapter, think of something you really *don't* want to do at all, something you have been actively putting off but you know will need to be done eventually.

I'm secretly hoping that you've chosen something so demotivating that being asked to think about it just now has made you feel guilty!

Apart from guilt, what feelings do you get when you think of doing that thing today or tomorrow.

Again, I bet none of those feelings are 'motivation'.

At this point, I can almost hear several of you say "Aha! Well that's where you're wrong Mr Smarty Pants! 'Lack of motivation' *was* one of the feelings I experienced, so there!"

Well Mr Smarty Pants says you are talking nonsense!

And he says that with confidence because, and this is important to understand . . . motivation is *not* a feeling.

PHANTOM FEELINGS

You have never *felt* motivated in your life. You will never, ever, in your whole existence, *feel* motivated. You can certainly *be* motivated and you can *get* motivated. You *can* motivate someone else, *find* motivation or *have* motivation.

But actually feel it? Nope, that's never going to happen.

When I asked you earlier to think of doing something you really love, the reasons you were motivated to do it will have been things like excitement, happiness, being with friends/family, fun, peace and quiet, or similar.

Your words may have been slightly different but each reason that you have to do that particular thing will be a word that describes a positive feeling.

When you thought of the reasons for not doing the thing you've been putting off, you probably used words like too boring, too difficult, not fun, too busy, don't know where to start, don't know if I'm doing it right or just simply can't be bothered.

Each of these words and phrases contains either a negative feeling or, at least, a lack of a positive feeling that makes the task seem difficult, energy sapping or simply moves it further and further down your list of priorities.

This 'lack of positive feeling' is what we actually mean when we say we 'lack motivation'.

It's important, especially in the world of teenagers, to note that there will often be a point, depending on what the task is that we are putting off, when the feelings of guilt will build to a point where they become too painful to ignore. We simply *have* to do it because, as you have learned, pain is one of our most powerful motivators.

The drive to avoid pain lies behind many classic teenager behaviours such as cramming sessions in the final hours before exams, tidying their room because a friend is coming round, or, as we discussed in chapter 2, doing anything solely because enough pain has been applied to make them do it.

To briefly sum this up:

motivation = presence of positive feelings
lack of motivation = lack of positive feelings *or* presence of negative feelings

A WHY'S MAN SAID

I'm sure few of us know any teenager who thinks "These dishes need washed. Woohoo, let me at 'em, this is going to be fun!" Actually, come to think of it, there are very few *adults* who would ever say this! There are certain household tasks that we all struggle to find the motivation to do and this is even more apparent with teenagers.

However, I *have* met a teenager who once told me she had happily been doing housework, vacuuming the living room to be specific, in the short space of time she had between getting home from school and leaving for her session with me.

In my experience, the relationship between teenagers and house-work is somewhat tempestuous and usually accompanied by long conversations about who's turn it is and how long it's going to take, so I must have looked surprised and probably a little bit impressed. She registered my reaction and explained, very calmly, "That's what you do in a family, everyone chips in and does their bit."

This is a perfect example of motivation.

She did it because making a contribution by completing that task makes her feel part of the family.

And this is what many parents fail to notice.

We get stuck on the '*what*' and we miss the importance of the '*why*'.

In all of our lives, *everything* we do needs a 'why'. Where that 'why' comes from and how important that why is to us will have a direct correlation to how long any motivation will last.

Being part of a family is a pretty important thing, especially to this young lady, and so that motivation is stronger than any cash reward. An attempt to motivate her to complete this task with money may still work but will be significantly shorter lived than if you take the time to understand her 'why'.

Like the responses to fear we looked at in chapter 4, I believe there are similarly clear levels of 'why'. The higher of the four levels you can achieve, the bigger the motivation and the greater your chance of success of getting the task done.

I guarantee you will already be using some, if not all of these levels already. But I would ask . . . are you using them on purpose and to the best effect?

The Levels of 'Why?'

Levels 1 & 2

Level 1 – Things

You know that feeling you get when, after putting it off for ages, you finally clean the inside of the car or cut the grass or clean out the cupboard where you keep all that important 'stuff' that you can't possibly throw away? You know that rush of satisfaction that happens just after you've done it, the task is complete and now everything in your life seems to be better for a little while?

Yeah, that feeling right there, that's the lowest level of 'why'.

As we go through the levels, you will see that each has an associated amount of energy (effort) required to be put in to make something happen and this directly relates to the amount of benefit (change) that comes back out as a result of that thing happening.

For example, at this lowest level, it takes very little effort and energy to clean the car[1] and that's why the level of change that comes back out, although feeling good at the time, doesn't last. The car will be messy again in a week – any change was very temporary.

LIVING IN A MATERIAL WORLD

When it appears that the only reason for a teenager to do something is to temporarily affect their immediate surroundings, you will find them searching for the answer to the Motivation Question,

Why should I?

---

[1] I will not accept any protestations here, it only takes the energy of getting yourself away from the telly for half an hour!

As we know, a teenager's immediate surroundings have very little effect on their life in general unless those surroundings directly impact the answers to the Two Teen Questions.

Why tidy their room if no-one is going to see it?

Why help clean the house if it's not their mess?

Why take care of their personal appearance if they don't care what they look like?

Why wash the dishes when there is no reward, thanks or praise?

Have you ever noticed that your teenager will happily spend a fortune (probably courtesy of you!) on clothes, makeup, jewelry and the latest technology then treat it as if it is worthless and throwaway?

Phones get broken, expensive clothes lie on the floor, jewelry gets lost, things get given away. They wanted these things so badly, so why do they place such little value on them once they have them?

I promise you it's not that they don't care. It's simply the initial energy that the item (i.e. the phone, the clothes, the earrings etc.) possessed fades very quickly and it becomes just another 'thing' that they have among their 'stuff'.

For example, they want the latest, fanciest phone to *fit in* with their pals, but once all their pals know they have the latest fanciest phone and have given it due praise and attention, it's just a phone.

It was that precious moment of fitting in and the feeling it gave them that your teenager craved. The phone was merely a vehicle to get them a little flood of dopamine, the chemical that is found in the brain's reward and pleasure centres. Dopamine is highly addictive, it's the same chemical that is released when we smoke, drink, take risks, go on thrill rides, gamble, break the rules and get loads of 'likes' on a social media post. It feels amazing . . . but not for very long. As it begins to wear off, your teenager wants, and may even *need*, more.

Now that everyone has seen it, the phone has lost its power. It's not going to attract any more praise or attention. However, a new laptop or that amazing jacket or tickets to that big concert that everyone is going to or . . .

The list is endless because these 'things' lack the energy to maintain the dopamine hit. I promise, if you attempt to motivate your teen this way, you'll spend a lot of money and achieve nothing. It's not the 'thing' they actually want, it's the feeling that having the 'thing' gives them.

Here's a common example I hear about all the time − offering money for doing well in exams, e.g. "I'll give you £50 for every 'A' you get."

Sound familiar? If you've tried it, how did it work for you?

For some teenagers, usually those who have a particular financial goal for a particular reason, e.g. an end of term holiday or festival, this approach *may* work but, for most, the offer of money for exam results produces a short burst of frenzied activity before quickly reverting into Level 1's apathy again. The money was an antidote to the fear. But it doesn't last.

The confused parent can't figure out where they've gone wrong. They remind their teenager about the tempting financial offer, suggesting all the 'things' they can buy with their new found riches, they tell them how they wish they were made such a generous offer when they were a teenager but it doesn't seem to motivate.

It's just money and without a 'why' to have that money, the reward does not have enough energy to maintain motivation through 6 months of hard work and study. Your teenager has likely never had a significant amount of disposable income and therefore, as money, it has no real value. It does have value if it buys them a way to fit in, be accepted or be someone, but we'll come to that a little bit later.

Here's a simple rule. . .

You will not motivate a teenager for any sustainable period of time with rewards of material things.

Let me revisit a common parental frustration we mentioned earlier, "Why does my teenager refuse to do any chores around the house?"

Simply explained, your house lacks *energy*. It's just 'the house', it's always been 'the house' and, as far as their experience tells them, it will always will be 'the house'. It's not going anywhere and if they don't do the chore, someone else will – they always have done. It's the same as turning the lights off when they leave a room . . . a simple task you would think. Apparently not for teenagers!

You may try saying things like 'do you know how much we pay for electricity?' But the mind of a teenager who has never had any experience or responsibility of paying bills, earning money or running a household can't relate to this at all.

To them, it's like you are talking a foreign language.

The material aspects of a teenager's world are fleeting. There will be many things held precious but the majority of 'things' are easily replaced and lack sufficient energy to create a long term change in levels of motivation.

If we want our teenagers to be motivated for longer than the brief rush they experience when their phone is shiny, new and hasn't yet got a massive crack in the screen[2], then we need to be much more creative in our approach.

But before we get to that creativity, let's look at what parents do when they discover, as they inevitably will, that these material tactics don't work?

An exasperated parent can temporarily lack clarity and understanding. Out of frustration, anger, anxiety or whatever, it's all too easy to fall back into old well worn parenting patterns.

In such situations and without necessarily being consciously aware, parents often retreat to a comfortable, familiar mindset that worked when their teenager was much younger. It requires very little energy and effort – only marginally more than buying them stuff – to take away the carrot and get the stick out instead.

It's time to lay some ground rules in this bloody house . . .

Level 2 – Control

A long time ago, I used to work for a call centre in one of the UK's big banks. I only did it for about 9 months but, in that time, I couldn't tell you the number of times I uttered the words 'Yes sir, I understand completely but our terms and conditions clearly state. . .'.

Have you ever had one of those conversations? When the person you are talking to seems rigid and stiff and won't budge from a set of arbitrary rules that, to you, mean absolutely nothing at all?

---

[2] Seriously, how do they keep doing that? Answers on a postcard please.

Have you ever been frustrated at the unwillingness of a 'jobsworth' to see reason and treat you like a human being? Or, even worse, someone who insists on quoting the rules over and over again even though they are written in such an ambiguous way that they could mean four different things to three different people?

That 'jobsworth' you were talking to might have been me!

Sorry.

BECAUSE I SAY SO . . .

In every walk of life, human beings have a simple process to help us influence people to conform and behave in a certain way. A process that is intended to give us control and make the world more predictable.

We make *rules*.

When you think about it, this makes total sense. Rules are pretty easy to make and, once they are established and written down for all to see, require almost no energy to maintain. The very existence of a rule *should* be sufficient to guarantee that everyone who reads it will follow it and, ultimately, do what you want them to do.

If these rules originate with a 'higher power' such as police, council, government, royalty, society or God, they can have significant influence and people are very likely to follow them. The 'higher power' becomes the 'why'.

It's because everyone follows the rules that we have the good fortune to live in this happy, united country where there is no crime and perfect behavior from every citizen. No-one is ever loud, drunk or obnoxious. Everyone knows what they should do and follows the rules to the letter. Everyone drives carefully within the speed limit, no-one ever steals an extra roll from the breakfast buffet (just to cover until lunch) and every recycling bin, in every neighbour-hood, is full of spotlessly clean and perfectly crushed plastics. . . . It's this way because there are rules.

And rules mean everyone does as they are told.

Except, as we all well know, they don't.

People get drunk, drive too fast and frequently smuggle a roll or two from the breakfast buffet.

People like the structure and security that rules give their day to day life but they typically don't follow them to the letter. As a moti-vational tool, rules are very low energy and really nothing more than a bunch of words. If someone wants to break a rule, they can, and will, do it easily. How many times have you heard the phrases, 'rules were made to be broken' and 'exception to the rules'? To call someone a 'rulebreaker' typically suggests admiration for them.

Why then do we, as parents, think that *our* rules are better rules than everyone else's rules and should be followed to the letter, without exception, no questions asked?

As we have seen, the teenage mind is focused on answering the Two Teen Questions, neither of which require parental acceptance. Any rules imposed on a teenager will need to have significant energy to have even the slimmest chance of being followed.

"Dad said to be home by 11pm at the latest but all my friends are staying out until 11:30. If I leave early I'll look silly, people will make fun of me and I might miss something exciting and fun, but if I stay out late Dad will go mental."

Which of those choices do you think has the greater power when a teen is deciding to be home on time or not? Which produces the greater energy for the teenager?

Now don't get me wrong, rules are very useful and are established with good reason.

For example, speed limits ensure that most people keep within a safe and reasonable speed and there are clear, understood penalties for breaking the rules. I think we can all agree that, in general terms, speed limits are a good thing.

But drivers will get annoyed about speed limits when they are caught doing 34mph in a 30mph limit, even though they know they have clearly broken the rules.

By contrast, drivers caught doing 55mph in a 30mph limit area tend to accept that it's a 'fair cop'. They understand they've gone too far and there will be a punishment, even though they've broken exactly the same rule as the driver doing 34 in a 30.

How is this different?

Some would argue it's a matter of context. That the rules need to be flexible and should 'bend' to take account of the specific situation.

This is how teenagers feel about parental rules.

But where do you stop bending. If 34mph is OK, is 35? And if 35 is OK then is 37? Where does the new line get drawn? If we let someone away with it once, is the rule just useless?

This is how parents feel about teenagers breaking parental rules!

In the mid 20th century, when buildings were getting higher and higher, engineers knew they had to protect their new 'skyscrapers' from the effects of wind. So they did what they thought was sensible, they made them solid, rigid and inflexible. Then along came earthquakes and typhoons and these wonders of modern technology simply crumbled.

It didn't take them long to work out what was wrong. Since that time, and a couple of expensive disasters, all tall buildings that you have ever climbed, seen or watched people BASE jump from are built to gently sway and flex.

Flexible buildings don't crumble when things shake them.

Neither do flexible parents.

The Rules for Rules

THE GOOD, THE BAD AND THE RGR

Here's a handy guide that will help with the process of setting rules. There are 3 different types of rules that you need to know about and, I suggest that while you read this, you ask which type you tend to set most often.

Bad Rules – First you need to know about bad rules so you can avoid making them! There are three elements to a bad rule.

1. *Bad Engineering.* Rules are often set to try and close a gap that is simply too wide or, in the eyes of your teenager, doesn't actually exist.

   For example, a teenager who is currently not studying at all is suddenly locked in their room and not allowed out until they know everything they need to know about quadratic equations. Or a teenager who has survived on chocolate and fizzy drinks for years is suddenly, and without warning, allowed nothing but salad and mineral water.

   Rules like these are expecting too much change in one un-expected, painful movement. They will almost definitely meet with resistance and fail to achieve the intended result.

2. *Gimme A Reason.* Another cause of resistance to rules comes from a lack of clarity as to *why* the rule has actually been set or what purpose it has.

   A rule that cannot be explained, will be ignored.

Why should your teenager follow a rule you can't explain? And even if you can explain it, what if they don't share your desired outcome?

What if they don't want to go to university? What if they want to study drama instead of science? What if they don't want their life to be the same as yours?

Can you explain to them *why* they should do it your way?

Would you obediently follow a workplace rule that seemed obstructive to your career plans and couldn't be justified or explained by your manager?

I don't think you would.

3. *We All Fall Down*. And finally, as we have discussed, a bad rule is inflexible and strictly enforced. If you dish out severe punishment every time a rule is broken, forgotten or not followed to the letter then you won't have a teenager who is learning about life, you will have a teenager who learns to obey out of fear.

We have a name for people who rule by enforcing fear.

We call them dictators.

By being a 'parental' dictator you are telling your teenager they have 3 choices; obey, escape or rebel.

Is that the kind of parent you want to be?

I didn't think so.

Let's try loosening the boundaries of our rules a little and see what happens. Let's put a little more flexibility in there . . .

Good Rules – Good rules have broadly the same three main elements as bad ones, just used in a very different way.

1. *A Reason For Being*. A good rule has a 'why' that is understood by *everyone* involved. A good rule has a good reason for being and, whether they like it or not, everyone 'gets' it.

2. *The Toilet Paper Test*. Everybody knows that a good toilet paper is soft and strong. This is also a good guide for your rules. Your rule should be strong enough to influence a change while at the same time being soft enough to allow time and space for the change to happen.

For example, moving your teen from one extreme of behaviour to the other can be introduced gradually, rather than imposed suddenly and without warning. A rule such as 'you will study for 3 hours a night' could be 'each week I'd like you to study for ten minutes more than you did the week before'.

Rather than clearing absolutely everything sugary out of the house and putting a ban on crisps you could make a six week plan to phase out various things one at a time, allowing some time to get used to it. This week we have fewer fizzy drinks, next week we cut out the crisps, the next week we cut chocolate by half. It may seem soft in the short term, but it is also strong with a specific goal in mind and a significantly higher chance of success in the longer term.

This rule passes the Toilet Paper Test.

3. *Quake Proof*. Sometimes even excellent drivers and very virtuous people creep up to 34mph in a 30mph area and don't notice. Should they be punished in the same way as someone who regularly drives at 55mph in the same area? Mistakes happen and a good rule needs the ability to bend and flex to give everyone some wiggle room.

I like the saying 'it isn't about how often you fall off the wagon, it's about how quickly you get back on'. If acceptance and understanding are the keys to change (and you know that they are!), a failure to study for more time than last week, or an evening where no study is done at all should be acknowledged but, for a first offence, shouldn't be punished.

Everyone involved accepts that the rule has been broken and understands that tomorrow we get back on it. If it is broken a second time then more discussion is required. A third time, and we are bending it a bit too much so repercussions should begin to appear.

If the rule continues to be broken then we need to look more closely at the rule itself. Why is it being broken? Often the reason a good rule isn't working is because it is failing one of these criteria. It doesn't have a good reason to be there, it fails the Toilet Paper test, it's too flexible or not flexible enough.

These are easy to address and as soon as you do, your good rule transforms into a *really* good rule almost instantly.

Really Good Rules – A really good rule (let's call this an RGR so we have our very own cool code) is just a good rule with one additional element (other than the word 'really').

Agreement.

A rule into which *everyone* has had an input and with which all agree will always be the easiest to maintain and enforce. If your teen has fully bought in to the rule, understands why it exists, what it means, accepts the positives of following it and accepts the repercussions of breaking it, then you will have a much simpler task to keep this rule working for everyone.

In fact, a mutually agreed rule has extra power simply due to the fact that your teenager was part of the team that set it up. They can't say they don't agree with any part of the rule and they can't even rebel against it properly as they would only be rebelling against themselves!

In fact, RGRs have a higher chance of working because they're not really just rules. They are also great examples of the third level of 'why' . . .

The Levels of 'Why?'

Levels 3 & 4

177 CRACKING THE TEEN CODE

Level 3 – Momentum

CAN YOU FEEL IT?

As we discussed earlier, every single thing we ever do will be motivated by our emotions and, as you'll know if you've read my first book,[3] I believe that our feelings are the key to our most powerful motivational forces.

Your teenager is currently in the middle of establishing their Emotional Code – a set of emotions and feelings, many of which they have learned from you, that tell them whether what they are currently doing or experiencing is right or wrong, good or bad, is working for them or hurting them.

They will be laying down codes for almost every decision in their lives – big stuff like relationships, money, career, family, health, as well as the smaller stuff such as fashion choices, diet, fitness, hairstyle and so on.

Motivation is easy when your teen believes their code has the potential to be fulfilled.

Motivation requires emotion.

Let's look at a couple of general teenage stereotypes to demonstrate how this works.

Typical Teen 1: Studies hard, is dedicated and motivated to do well in their exams, spends lots of time at home, sometimes struggles to talk to people they don't know, is very quiet in almost all social situations.

---

[3] Costello, B. *Breakthrough: A Blueprint for your Mind*. Glasgow: Riverclyde Books, 2016. www.rcbks.com/breakthrough

Typical Teen 2: Says they want a 'good' job, enjoys being with friends, struggles to focus on study, confident with almost anyone, hardly ever spends time in the house but is always there and smiling at big family occasions.

There are some common parental questions associated with these two scenarios.

For Teen 1: Why can't they make friends as easily as Teen 2? Why do they hold themselves back in social situations even though they are so bubbly and easy-going around the family? Why are they so anxious about what people think of them? Don't they realise that they can't possibly be the best at everything?

For Teen 2: Why can't they motivate themselves to study? How can they say they want a good job then put no effort into actually getting one? Why is it that they would rather be out partying all the time when they are so clever and could really go places? Can't they see they are threatening their whole future?

These common parental questions also have a range of common parental answers.

The most common answers that I hear in these situations are that Teen 1 is socially anxious and shy while Teen 2 is lazy and throwing their life away.

In fact, neither of these answers are true.

If you look at the descriptions again and read between the lines, both these teens are very motivated. They are just motivated to do different things in very different ways, but believe it or not, by *exactly* the same things!

They are motivated by external factors triggering their emotional code. These feelings are more commonly known as *values*.

Let's look at these two codes and see if you can tell who's who.

Code 1	Code 2
Being liked	Being liked
Success	Fun
Family	Excitement
Excitement	Success
Fun	Family

What do you think?

You'll notice that the feelings on both 'codes' are exactly the same, but they are in a slightly different order and that tiny difference is more than enough to produce two very different personalities.

No-one is motivated by things.
No-one is motivated by rules.
Everyone is motivated by emotions.

You can *only* motivate people by fulfilling their emotional code. If you can't work out that code, or you actively choose to ignore it, I promise that someone or something else will win the motivational battle for your teen every single time.

Our party animal teenager isn't lazy, they want to be liked and, in their head, it's much easier to be liked at a party than it is reading a book.

In the same way, our other teen isn't actually shy, they just value being liked so much, the fear of *not being liked* overwhelms them. They find that they can't speak to people they don't know, just in case they say something stupid, ridiculous or make a fool of themselves some other way.

In fact, for Teen 1, not being liked could be seen as failure and that would also break the second feeling in their code, the desire for success, and cause even more pain.

It's pretty clear from these examples that our quieter, more studious teen is more likely to be Code 1. They are more motivated by success and family than fun and excitement, therefore the choice of studying hard, exam success and the chance of University is an easy choice for them. Success is more important than fun – they will work hard to achieve, and fun can come later.

However, placing such importance on success also brings a lot of pressure. If they fail an exam, their success is threatened and they will feel that. Imagine, after an unexpectedly poor result, a well-meaning parent shows disappointment or surprise at the failed exam. For years the 'normal' for their teen has been great results – this may just be a one off blip, but now we have the top three aspects of their code in jeopardy. They have *failed* to succeed, they have *failed* at family and they have *failed* to be liked.

That's an emotional kick in the teeth, isn't it? Before you know it, the whole house of cards comes crashing to the ground. The emotional pain can be significant and all from one failed exam and an innocent parental reaction of surprise and disappointment.

I hope you are beginning to see why I am passionate about parents understanding the emotional landscape of teenager's personality.

In my experience, too many parents treat their children like robots when they are living, breathing, emotional 'adults-in-training'. The more we understand that our teenagers are caught somewhere between adult and child, the more chance we have of motivating them to become the happy, content grown-ups we desperately want them to be.

When we understand this, it becomes clear that Teen 2 isn't lazy. It's just that, as we look at them right now, they are far more motivated by fun and excitement than they are by success.

In a dilemma between the two, fun is going to win every time. Combine that with wanting to be liked and we have a fun, confident joker who gets much more emotional validation from being around people than he or she does from exam results.

CRACKING THE CODE

So what do we do? Do we just leave things alone? Do we just accept that there is nothing we can do, throw in the parenting towel and allow our 15 year old to party their way through school?

No, of course we don't.

What we do is use a little bit of psychology to begin motivating our teenagers in new, more effective ways.

If we can match our 'why' to our teen's code, we will have tapped into an incredible energy.

Remember the teenager I told you about earlier who did housework because 'that's what you do in a family'? From this we can reasonably assume that 'family' is pretty high up in her code. When faced with a decision between prioritising family or friends, family will win on almost all occasions.

Uncovering and giving her parents that understanding was enough for them to be able to tie all manner of tasks into 'family' and get her motivated in many aspects of life.

See how that works?

So for this teenager, if . . .

Doing housework = Helping out = **Family** = **Motivated** = Stairs vacuumed

then . . .

Working hard in school = Parental pride = **Family** = **Motivated** = Studying teenager

Do you know what's important to *your* teen?

When they make a decision, who or what wins? If you can learn to look past superficial, material things and consider their deeper, unconscious emotional needs e.g. a new flashy phone means I will fit in and people will want to be my friend. If you can identify those needs and recognize what it is that they really want emotionally, then you will have access to some of the most powerful motivational energy around.

This is why RGRs work. When you set a rule without agreement it will be one sided and almost guaranteed to be meeting only one set of needs, most likely yours. That's why you're so motivated for the rule; it has *your* 'why' written into it!

However, if your teenager has been a participant in the creation process of the RGR, their agreement means that the rule will not only meet your emotional needs but, far more importantly from the perspective of motivating *them*, it will meet theirs. That balance has the energy required to turn a rule into something that may just work.

RGRs have *everyone's* agreement and meet *everyone's* needs so *everyone* is motivated to make them work.

You'll now understand that your teen *is* motivated to do lots of things, it's just not always the things that you want them to do! All the things they are doing, even if it is gaming, eating, partying, drinking, smoking or any of the other apparently negative behaviours that you are now witnessing, are all driven and motivated by their hidden emotional Teen Code.

However, one thing that is true of all teenagers is that the Teen Code, unlike the Parental Code, is not 'set'. It is still soft and pliable and that means one thing . . . there is still time.

Level 4 – Mission possible

What if there is an *ultimate* 'why'.

A 'why' which has started, and ended, wars. A 'why' which has led to some of the most amazing achievements of the entire human race. A 'why' that changes everything.

This is the 'why' of *mission*.

It has many names, some people call it their 'higher purpose', 'higher power' or 'life's work' and others a 'calling' or 'reason for being'. Whatever it is called, it's a 'why' with enough power to motivate us to make sacrifices and work harder than we could have ever imagined in the pursuit of its fulfillment.

Imagine if Teen 2 ('party' teen) went along to a careers event at school one day and got chatting to a representative from a university. They hit it off and this person (as far as our teen is concerned) says all the right things, in the right way, at the right time. They talk about how amazing Uni will be, the people they will meet, the activities that are available and how much fun going to study in this amazing place can be. Suddenly, Teen 2 comes to believe they have everything it takes to study at one of the top universities in the country, decide that's exactly what they want and can't think of anything else.

Imagine the effect on their code when this becomes their prime focus. It's not just a goal or desirable outcome that they want to somehow work in a rough direction towards.

It's much bigger than that.

It's their *mission*.

Imagine how easy it would be to motivate them to do pretty much anything if it would help them in the pursuit of that mission.

Of the Two Teen Questions, it is the identity-based 'who am I?' which is most closely tied into the concept of mission. Our mission is not something we just do, it shows the world *who we are*.

And if you can work out who you are, what your mission is and what you need to do to achieve it, everything changes.

Sounds amazing, doesn't it?

But there is hard work ahead – changes and sacrifices will be required.

A teenager with a determination to study at University can end up putting lots of pressure on themselves as they sacrifice many things in the pursuit of that mission.

I have met teens with limited social lives, extensive extra-curricular CVs full of volunteering opportunities and other amazing achievements, and a determined focus to achieve a particular outcome in their lives. They want to achieve their mission.

In the same way, I have worked with young people involved in elite sport and listened as they tell me the lives they live in the pursuit of their dream. They never give up, they accept change and sacrifice, they follow instruction and coaching and all for one reason. They want to complete their mission.

Let me share a personal example here. Many years ago, when I found out I was going to be a dad for the first time, my sole focus was on being a 'good dad' and, to me, that meant providing for my family.

This very quickly became my *mission*.

Within a matter of only a few months I had radically overhauled my social life, changed my circle of friends, changed job and had, for the first time in my life, started on a path to an actual career. In short, everything I did became about looking after this little human being I had helped create even though I hadn't even met him or her yet.[4]

To me, none of those things ever felt like a sacrifice.

To me, it was just 'who I am'.

There was never a single doubt in my mind that everything I changed, every 'friend' I stopped talking to, every interview I attempted, every shirt, tie and pair of proper grown up shoes I put on, every friend who heard me say "no, I'm not coming", every sacrifice I made, was entirely and completely worth it.

Now, 18+ years later, I'm still on that mission and everything I've done in the intervening years and continue to do – from starting my own business to saving for our dream house, from having

---

[4] And 18 years later, that little human being would write the foreword to this book!

sunny holidays to getting fit – were driven by a mission to provide for my family.

I never questioned any of them, it was always a matter of how and when they *would* be achieved.

This is the power of mission.

The drive that mission creates is so powerful and has so much energy, we will bounce back from every setback, every disappointment, every mistake, and we will, without hesitation, get up and go after it again.

And again.

And again.

And again.

This powerful drive is what sets a mission apart from a goal.

I have met many teenagers who have the *goal* of being professional football players. In Scotland where I live, it is the dream of many young boys and, increasingly, girls.

Some are really good players who play for their school or a local club team and maybe a couple of scouts from the big teams have been to watch them play. It's all very exciting to be 15 and in demand, and they work hard to keep in the scout's eye.

But then they get older, they move up an age group, training is on a Friday night when they'd rather be partying and the scouts haven't been in touch lately. They begin to draw their own conclusions from this – maybe they're not as good as they thought and they should just give up on the dream, knuckle down and get in to university or get a job?

But one young guy I met recently was different. When all his friends were planning to go to college or university after school, he decided he wasn't going to apply for further education because he was certain he was going to play football. No question in his mind.

Quietly and without fuss he wrote a personal letter to every single professional club in the whole of the UK asking for an opportunity, detailing his skills, his experience and his desire to play football for a living.

While he waited patiently for replies, he continued to train in the gym and on the pitch, in all weathers, five or six times a week. He continued to hold the sole focus that football was his future. Nothing would divert him from his mission. It was only a matter of time until someone wrote back.

And he was right.

At the time of writing he has moved away from his family and friends and has a contract with a Scottish professional club. He's doing really well, is willing to learn and is working hard to progress through the ranks.

Of course he's working hard. He's in pursuit of his mission.

By contrast, I once met a guy who declared, with a completely straight face, that he was going to be the manager of one of the top football teams in the English Premiership within 10 years. I suggested that, at the age of 28, currently unemployed, living with his girlfriend's parents in Glasgow and (this is important) almost zero football experience, this might be a tall order!

This illustrates a really important aspect of any mission that parents should help teenagers understand.

Your mission needs to be something you can actually do!

If you have never picked up a tennis racket before the age of 25, are slightly overweight and struggle to get to the top of the stairs without being horribly out of breath then being Wimbledon Champion in the next 5 years is probably not a realistic mission. That's not to say that you can't work hard and become a really, really good tennis player. It's just that, outside of a Hollywood screenplay, there is no chance of winning a grand slam tournament!

I believe we should always be ambitious but at the same time we need to be, at least a little, realistic!

Give a mission every chance it can possibly have to thrive and grow and sometimes all the mission needs is a tweak, a slight change of focus to make it entirely possible.

If you can't play football, can you coach football?

If you can't be a doctor could you help people be healthier some other way?

If you can't be an actor could you still do something else in the entertainment industry?

There are always, always choices. As parents it is often our job to find them so that the mission never dies.

MIRROR, MIRROR . . .

To close this chapter I want you to ask yourself a series of questions about your teenager. Take a few minutes to consider these questions and the answers you give to them.

1. What motivates them?
   Friendship? Success? Happiness? Family? Shutting out fear?

2. What you are doing to help motivate them?
   Shouting? Talking? Helping?

3. What level of 'why' are they on?
   Are they looking for a good job, so they can earn enough money to buy that car they want, or are they driven by a mission to make a difference in the world?

Your answers may well lead to some deeper questions.

Ask yourself, are they looking for low energy returns of the material world – addicted to short, term dopamine highs such as game achievements and owning shiny new things?

Are they controlled by rules, trapped between pleasure and pain, unable to decide for themselves as they have to constantly ensure they are doing the 'right' thing?

Have they finished setting their code? And, if they have, is it helping them or are they trying to fulfill their code in ways that are hurting them? What does their code look like?

Are they riding on the energy of a mission, dedicated and focused as they drive themselves towards something they believe is not only what they want, but is *who they are*? And, if they are on mission, is the mission realistic?

And notice that the four levels of 'why' also have a maturity indicator built in.

Babies are not born dedicated to achieving a mission, they just need to be cared for and have things done for them. Children need rules to know what they should and shouldn't do. Teenagers have a need to answer their Two Teen Questions. If we are lucky, by the time they become young adults, they will find their mission and focus on making it a reality.

Every day I meet adults who have no mission in life and still don't know who they are. The root cause almost always lies in their teenage years and, more often than not, is connected to their relationship with their parents.

**As a parent, you have the opportunity
to change your teen's future.**

You have the knowledge to nurture a mission.

Now, let me ask one final important question that leads us into the next chapter;

Do you allow your teen to *fully* express themselves and to be who they want to be?

As parents, we know exactly what it feels like to live through the confusion of our teenage years. It's important that we remember that not all mistakes are equal and not everything that lies outside our 'normal' is a mistake.

In fact, many of the situations we call mistakes are more like scientific experiments and there is an important rule in science – that *every* result tells us something.

And now you are an amazing parent who is accepting and understanding there are some simple things to remember as we go forward.

Discuss before you decide.

Be a leader, not a dictator.

Be like toilet paper.

Chapter 5 – What The . . . ?

- You will never feel motivated. Motivation is the result of meeting an emotional code that drives us to do the things we want to do.

- Every action needs a 'why'. If it doesn't have one then nothing will happen. If there isn't a reason to do something . . . we won't!

- There are 4 levels of Why:
  - it will get me stuff
  - it's the rules
  - it feels good
  - it's who I am

  The last two are where the motivation lies.

- You have 3 choices when setting a rule:
  - Bad Rules you make yourself
  - Good Rules are flexible and pass the toilet paper test
  - Really Good Rules are Good Rules which also have the agreement of everyone involved.

- Your teenager is on a mission to find a Mission. Listen, pay attention and help them find their path. This path will lead to success.

6

Too Much, Too Young

When I look back on my teenage years, I remember that I really enjoyed being alone. I was a teenage boy in the early years of home computers and could easily spend hours playing computer games.

I would spend weekends wandering Glasgow's (in)famous Barras Market, buying cheap, pirated versions of the latest games (shhhh, don't tell) and rushing home with the anticipation of a new adventure.

Gaming was my thing.

I remember the excitement of putting the tape in the machine[1], the anticipation as lines danced on the screen and screechy noises gave signal that something positive was happening. However, I also remember how many times the game failed at the last minute or crashed as soon as I started it up.

Frequent failure meant unfulfilled excitement and of course another visit for a replacement but to be honest it never really mattered. The journey, the anticipation, even the failure was all part of the experience.

But I wasn't alone all the time. I had many friends and spent a lot of time inside and outside of school hours with Dave, who shared

---
[1] The ZX Spectrum 128K +2 if you must know.

my love of pool and arcade games, and Jim, who shared my love of wandering about doing very little!

This was my teenage life.

However, in my school life, I was attracting unwanted attention that, due to a distinct lack of experience and no effective models, I really didn't know how to handle. I was lucky because my experience of bullying was never really that bad. A bit of name calling, occasional tiny bursts of violence but the reason it is here in the book is because of what was happening inside my mind at the time.

I remember feeling as if I had no control, no choice in the matter. This was happening to me and, as far as I was concerned, I was powerless to stop it.

So I did nothing. I just let it happen.

But here is the point – when school finished for the day, I left all that behind. I would go home to my family, play football with my brothers and their friends or, at weekends, hang around with Dave and Jim. My computer games, the trips to get them, football, my friends were a safe, secure refuge, a million miles away from the pressures and fears of school.

Teenagers these days have no refuge.

The modern teenager never escapes the social pressures of school.

Never.

Your teenager leaves school at the end of the day and the whole world comes home with them . . . on social media. Your teenager carries the bullies along with their friends on the device in their pocket and *you* are paying for it to happen!

When we were at school, if we made a fool of ourselves, five people saw it, a few more people heard about it and then it was done.

In your teenager's world, any embarrassing event (or at least the aftermath) will almost certainly have been photographed or captured on video. Within minutes, not only does the whole school know it happened, they've *seen* it happen. And, if the clip is really violent, funny or humiliating, every school in the area will see it and who knows how far it will go from there? Viral video shows on TV are full of what happens when these clips leave the control of the person taking them.

A BRAVE NEW WORLD

The world our teenagers experience is *not* the same world we grew up in.

Our children carry their world in their pocket.

We can see, speak and interact with anyone, anywhere and learn anything in seconds. To our teenagers, a video call to the other side of the world to speak to a relative or friend is entirely normal. A friend of mine recently posted on social media that her seven year old daughter was on a video call with two friends. She was in Glasgow, one friend was in Saudi Arabia and the other in South America!

Seven years old!

When we were seven years old, video calling around the world was science fiction!

It is amazing that our children have the opportunities to become more aware of the world they live in and make so much of their lives. However, as much as the technology accelerates their intellectual and social growth, their *emotional intelligence* is not growing at the same rate.

They have full access to an adult world without any of the emotional tools to handle it.

Their emotions are still stuck in teenager mode.

Like most of you, when I was a teenager, my parents knew what I watched on TV because we only had one. They also knew who my main group of friends were and had met most if not all of them at some stage.

Can you say the same for your teenager? Do you know all (or even more than a handful) of their 1,500 facebook 'friends'? Do you know who their favourite YouTuber is, what they are posting on Instagram or who their Snapchat streaks are with?

Do you know who is influencing your teenager?

Many of your teen's models are not even 'real' people. The media explosion has surrounded us with myriad public facades constructed by YouTubers, vloggers, and celebrities. The world of social media and reality TV is made of distorted snapshots of 'fake' life, illusions of a perfect 'normality'. Without the experience to know anything else, can your teenager spot what is real and what is fake?

I know I am being a little dramatic. For balance, let me say that I honestly believe that the modern world is giving our children, of all ages, the chance to experience and engage with a range of views, personalities and belief systems that can only enhance their development and improve the world.

The chance for any growing mind to be exposed to a world of opposing thoughts and emotions is an amazing thing. But that growing mind also has to know how to handle it.

When the proverbial hits the fan, parental blindness is no excuse. You can't hide from it, you can't pretend it's not happening and, frustratingly, you can't fight it. You can't blame the internet, the school, their friends, Snapchat or anything else if your teen buckles under the pressure.

Yes, it is because of the modern world that our teens are under so much pressure, but it's not the modern world's fault.

The only way your teen could avoid it would be to cut off all sources of exposure to social media. But then how would they 'fit in'?

This is how it is.

And if you fight with reality, you will lose. Every time.

We live in a world driven by information and technology and you have a teenager with a huge unconscious desire to 'fit in'. It's only going to get weirder.

SHE CANNAE TAKE MUCH MORE, CAPTAIN

Because your teenager can't escape the world around them if they want to fit in, we need to start monitoring for any moment when the world becomes too much. The good news is that's pretty easy to do because it's impossible for anyone to hide everything, all the time.

All minds leak. Especially teenage ones. And when they leak, all we need to do is spot the emotional puddle.

We can sort most teenage emotions into three categories – **Anxiety, Stress** and **Depression**.

These are obviously not the only emotions they feel but focusing on these three is useful as it allows us to talk broadly about emotional experience and, importantly, how to help.

Remember, when your teen displays emotions, this does not mean they are 'broken'. The mind does nothing by accident and that means, if any of these emotions are on display, the mind has a damn good reason for them being there.

Your job is never to dismiss, belittle or ridicule that emotion.

Your job is to help someone you love find a better way to cope and to do that you have to understand how they got themselves into this mess in the first place.

Each emotional category has its own set of physical and verbal clues (aka 'the puddle') and these are fairly easy to spot if you know what to look for. I am not suggesting that the occasional use of a particular word or phrase or a single outburst of emotion means you need to rush your teenager off for psychological help.

We are, as always, looking for *patterns*, because each emotional state is just another one of life's dances.

We have looked at anxiety fairly extensively in the last two chapters and those puddles should now be relatively easy to spot. With that in mind, let's look at how to spot the puddles of stress and depression and complete the set.

Spotting Stress

There are many different levels of stress.

On Monday, choosing what to eat for dinner may be a simple and fun dilemma for your teenager, easily solved by listening to the options and choosing something.

But on Tuesday, it can be a whole different story. A simple request to make a choice can lead to a full blown meltdown with finger pointing, accusations over who loves who more, topped off with our now fully expected door slamming and prolonged 'silent treatment'.

Why do these two identical situations produce completely different reactions?

This is a stress puddle!

Let's do a little test . . .

You can either answer this question out loud or do it quietly, inside your head (so that the other people on the bus don't think you have lost your marbles!). Whichever way you prefer, DO NOT write anything down and don't ask anyone else.

Ready?

For the next 20 seconds I want you to think of as many different types of breakfast cereal as you can and count how many you get.

How did you do?

Unless you cheated, you'll have discovered that it's not as easy as you thought!

No matter what you use to run this test – breakfast cereals, cars, people, things to do or even a selection of dinner choices – the average number of answers that people come up with is usually between five and eight.

Even though we know that there are many more possible answers, under pressure a certain point is reached where our minds go all fuzzy and no more information can be squeezed in.

This feeling of blankness is commonly called 'overwhelm'.

The psychologist George Miller showed that our short-term memory only has room for 'seven plus or minus two' pieces of information before it all goes a little wonky (my word, not his).[2] Basically, your mind runs out of space when it is holding somewhere between five and nine pieces of information.

If a new piece of information appears, the mind needs to either throw away an old piece of information to make space for it or simply ignore the new piece and keep what it already has.

This process of space management uses a lot of energy and focus, leaving no room for any other thoughts. But the problem is that more thoughts just keep on coming. They don't stop. Your mind gets itself into a near endless decision cycle, trying it's best to remember everything but finding space very, very hard to come by. You will begin to forget things because all the space is used up. This adds to the pressure which takes up more space and so on and so on. It becomes increasingly difficult to cope and, if we have a memory slip and it's someone or something important that we've forgotten, we use more space feeling guilty about the fact that we've forgotten in the first place!

Imagine that this cycle goes on for even just a few days.

---

[2] Miller, GA. (1956) The magical number seven, plus or minus two: some limits on our capacity for processing information. *Psychol Rev.* 63(2):81–97.

This is stress.

It's hard enough for an adult, with a life that tends to be relatively well structured and compartmentalised. If we have a steady job, stable relationships, established financial situation and people tend to act in predictable ways then stress isn't a huge factor because we have plenty of mind space.

None of that is true for a teenager. Teenagers are juggling . . .

- relationships
- social politics
- hormones
- homework
- fitting in
- endless gossip
- romance
- career confusion
- gender confusion
- new emotions that don't have names
- changing friendships
- fashion pressure
- parent pressure
- sibling pressure

And remember, the modern world means that many of these things are with them, taking up space, every minute of every day.

We haven't included the pressure of learning all their academic subjects and the associated exams. Or the fact that every adult around them is adamant that failure in any of those exams means their whole future will be ruined.

Now you can understand how an innocent question about what you want for dinner is easily one decision too many!

In modern life, it's clear that 'overwhelm' is not only probable, it's inevitable. However, it is also completely manageable and, let's be honest, a little stress is a good thing.

When we are comfortable, we don't grow. It would be poor parenting to completely shield our teenagers from stress – it is much better to help them manage it.

And that's not that difficult to do.

For example, it is absolutely possible to name more than 20 breakfast cereals in 20 seconds if you have learned to use your mind properly. The same skill that would give you an entirely useless talent of cereal naming can help your teenager deal with the pressures of modern life.

HIERARCHY OF IDEAS

The first step is to understand not all thoughts are equal.

I had a recent conversation with a young man called Kevin about friendships and 'fitting in'. His Dad brought him to see me as he was, at the young age of 14, very stressed about various aspects of life. We quickly discovered a particular concern about one group of friends.

Kevin described how they had been friends since they were young but things had changed in the last couple of years. Now these boys would make fun of him for his shoes and his jeans because, unlike them, he didn't wear expensive labels. He very eloquently explained how, in his mind, labels weren't important and his trainers, bought from a local supermarket, were absolutely sufficient for what they did. "I don't need Nikes to tell people who I am", he said.

To his friends however, the Nike label and others were important. Anyone who didn't wear them was not part of the group and would be ridiculed. Including Kevin.

It was interesting to listen to him talk of his struggle to fit in to the group, a struggle that had been going on for just short of three years.

Let's be very clear, that's three years of stress trying to be accepted by a group of boys that he no longer agreed with on a fundamental issue of teenage life.

My question to him was simple, why do you keep trying to fit in with a group of guys you obviously don't like?

It was clear Kevin's emotional code did not place much, if any, value on fashion labels and he was definitely not a person who would ever strengthen his identity through making others feel small. I asked him why he was making this group such a priority in his mind? Why was he allowing them to fill so much space in his head when there were so many other amazing things he could choose to think about instead?

Why was he giving all his energy away?

These simple questions created some space in the stress for Kevin. It was clear, these boys were no longer his 'type' of friend. Much as it was an honourable endeavor to try to fit in and help them understand that they could change, it was also likely to be a frustrating and fruitless task. Kevin didn't blame them for being this way, but he remembered who they used to be and wished they were still like that.

We talked about keeping the door open to future possibilities, how this may just be a phase and things may settle back to the way the were. We talked about forgiveness. As we talked, Kevin's stress levels visibly began to change.

He told me about other friends who seemed more compatible with his own emotional code and, by the time we had finished the session, Kevin had decided that he had wasted too much time on the 'old' friends and it was time to move on with his life.

All I did was help him step back from his thoughts and get them in order. I helped him see things more clearly and deal with a stressful situation calmly and rationally. He learned that it was possible to make the stressful thoughts and feelings take up less space in his head.

He learned that some thoughts, when we really look at them, aren't as important as they pretend to be.

The space that was created can now be used for other things. Like choosing what he wants for dinner without getting upset about it.

EMPTYING THE TANK

Let's be clear though. Not every situation has such a clear cause as Kevin's.

Sometimes the teenage mind is less Six O'Clock News and more Game of Thrones. It's not necessarily a well organised series of events, presented in a linear way that makes total sense, There's often a vast array of characters, politics, infighting, treachery and people you've not heard about in years who suddenly appear back in the story out of nowhere.[3]

---

[3] I'm going to call this phenomenon 'doing a Gendry', though if you've never seen the show you'll have no idea what I'm talking about, so my apologies!

We need some sort of tool to get everything in order, neatly prioritised and well organised.

Luckily that tool is just a simple everyday paper and pencil.[4]

If you are really committed to helping your teen then you (and they) will make time for this exercise.

If your teenager tells you this is stupid, pointless or they don't have time, please refer back to the techniques in previous chapters. It may take a little coaxing to get them to sit still for a while but, if you can get them to at least give it a shot, less than an hour will do it.

It would be really good if you can *both* make the time to be 100% present, i.e. no phones, no distractions. Your undivided attention will be needed to keep them focused enough to pop the stress bubble.

Sit them down, grab a sheet of paper and mark out these five areas in circles.[5]

1. School
2. Friends
3. Family
4. Out of school activities
5. Other

Now simply ask your teen to list *all* the things that are currently running through their mind when they think about these categories.

---

[4] Paper and pencil is absolutely fine, but you might find this easier using one of the many excellent mindmapping apps available.
[5] Feel free to add any other categories appropriate to your teen. I've made a video clip of a worked example which can be found at http://rcbks.com/teenexample.

At first, expect comments like, "There's too much" or "It's just *everything*".

Ask them to focus on starting somewhere, the trickle will become a flood and your sheet will fill up pretty quickly.

Expect them to jump from one place to another, but just let them talk. And as they talk, you place everything into the different categories and, where there is a link across the sections together you can draw lines or arrows or anything that helps visually connect the growing 'map'.

The *only* other thing you do while they are talking is say, "Good, anything else?" and nod supportively.

Resist the urge to *fix* anything and don't get sidelined into discussing anything they say in detail.

Just listen, without judgment or comment, and encourage them to keep going. Don't be surprised if there are occasional tears.

Keep asking, keep writing and keep drawing lines and, before long, you will have many more than nine things on your sheet of paper.

To reduce stress and begin the process of change, simply show your teen the list and explain to them about the limited space in our minds. Once they understand that they cannot do everything at once, no matter how amazing they are, go through their map and score each entry from 1 (not important) to 10 (essential).

Check if there is anything that has obviously been blown out of proportion (as in Kevin's example) or if there are any issues which could be sorted, completed or changed almost instantly? Is there anything you, as a parent can do to help with lightening the load?

You know that cupboard in your house you don't want to open because it's overflowing with junk? It might be the same one that you promised back in chapter 5 you were going to clear by next week?

How amazing did it feel when you emptied it all out, got rid of all the crap you didn't need, put the important things back neatly and then bragged to everyone about how much extra space you had created?[6]

Well, this exercise is the mental equivalent of that process. It is easier to understand *why* we get stressed when we can clearly see *what* is causing it. And once we can see *what* is causing it, it is much easier to actually do something about it.

Stress is inevitable but it doesn't have to be a negative.

Some simple mind training is all that is needed to manage, organise and prioritise the causes of stress and now you know how to do it.

Go for it! Try out your new skills. It will be like having a new person in the house, I promise!

But what happens if that stress has twisted into something else? What if no mind map is going to be enough to clear the cloud hanging over your teen?

You can still help. It just needs a different type of thinking.

---

[6] What do you mean you don't know because you haven't done it yet . . . come on, I thought you were setting an example here!

Dealing with Depression

If you, or anyone you know, has ever experienced depression then you will be aware of how debilitating it can be. You'll also know how amazing it would be if, in the depths of the dark times, someone could give you just a little bit of control over what was going to happen next.

Well I am going to promise that you can.

In my opinion, depression is not an illness.

A person experiencing depression is not sick, they are *stuck*.

CAN I BE IN GROUP 1 PLEASE?

In the late 1960s and 70s, a series of controversial experiments were conducted by renowned psychologist Martin Seligman.[7] While investigating some theories about depression, he wondered if it was possible for depression to be 'taught'?

Seligman's team divided a large pack of dogs into three groups which he rather imaginatively called Group 1, Group 2 and Group 3. Every Group 1 dog had a Group 2 and a Group 3 partner so a dog from each group would always come in to the experiment together.

Briefly and with some simplification, here is how the experiments worked.

---

[7] Seligman, MEP. (1972) Learned helplessness. *Ann Rev Med*. 23(1):407–412.

Before I go into more detail about Seligman's work and his findings, I should warn you that his work was based on some rather cruel experiments with dogs. This section may be uncomfortable reading for some and, if you'd rather not read it, skip now to the grey panel on page 211 where I'll summarise it for you.

Group 1 dogs were strapped into a harness. They were left to chill out.

Group 2 dogs were also strapped into a harness before being placed in a box. The box was large enough to be comfortable but small enough to prevent the dogs from turning round.

Once inside the dogs were given electric shocks administered by electrifying the floor of the box. The shocks would last varying lengths of time ranging from half a second to five, six or even seven seconds. The dogs had no way to escape from the shocks but there was a small lever in the box which, if pushed, would stop each individual shock instantly. The dogs had to discover this lever for themselves but, being intelligent animals, most of them quickly worked it out.

And then we have poor Group 3. Group 3 were given exactly the same electric shocks, at exactly the same time, as their buddies in Group 2 but with one crucial difference. They couldn't stop their shocks.

They were in identical looking boxes, held in identical harnesses with the same electrified floor. They even had a lever but poor Group 3 would find that their lever was disconnected. When a Group 3 dog pushed their lever, nothing happened.

Unknown to the Group 3 dogs, everything about their experience was being controlled by Group 2. When the Group 2 dog pushed their lever and stopped their shock, they also stopped it for their friend in Group 3. However, to the oblivious Group 3 dogs, the pain of the shocks and then the relief when the shocks stopped, appeared to be entirely random.

Group 3 had no control over anything that was happening to them.

After the experiment had been carried out several times, a pattern was created. All the dogs, in all the groups, became familiar with what was happening and so repeated sets of predictable results were obtained; Group 2 dogs became quicker and quicker at pressing the lever and stopping the shocks, Group 3 dogs stopped doing anything at all because there was no point and Group 1 dogs sat in their harness, looking around, wondering why they were even there.

And then, once the pattern had been established, the experiment was changed.

Group 1 were now placed in the same boxes as the other dogs (with a working lever) however the boxes had been very slightly altered. A small hatch had been opened in the wall creating an opening between two chambers. This hatch would allow the dog to quickly and easily escape into a previously hidden part of the box where the floor was not electrified and they would be safe from the pain.

Here's what happened.

Group 1 dogs, having never been shocked before, had no idea what was going on and instantly made a break for the second chamber to get away from the source of the pain.

Group 2 dogs, after a very short while, stopped pushing the lever and, when they realised they had a way out, took the escape route as quickly as they could.

Group 3 dogs lay down, accepted the pain and whined as they were shocked repeatedly at random intervals. They made no attempt to escape through the open hatch right in front of them and since the Group 2 dogs had now escaped, there was no-one left to push the lever. For the poor Group 3 dogs, the pain only got worse.

For readers who chose to skip the details, here's a brief summary.

Of the three groups of dogs that Seligman and his team used, two were taught to have control over a painful stimuli. These two groups were first of all given a way to turn any pain off and then they were offered full escape from the source of any discomfort. In each case, both Group 1 and Group 2 took their escape quickly and without hesitation.

However, in the first part of the experiment, Group 3 were given no control over the stimuli. Their discomfort was being controlled by outside forces (in reality, the actions of Group 2). When the researchers offered Group 3 the chance to escape none of Group 3 took it. They refused escape from the source of their pain.

This phenomenon was called *learned helplessness*. The team of researchers had succeeded in 'teaching' depression.

Now, I have to say that I am not impressed by Seligman's methods at all,[8] but what he discovered is, in my opinion, one of the most

---

[8] His later work with humans responding to the unpleasant stimulus of annoying sounds was much more humane!

important psychological insights of modern times. The Group 3 dogs had learned that nothing they could do would change their circumstances so they just lay down and accepted their fate.

Even when escape was offered they couldn't understand they now had the ability to choose. They stayed as they were and endured the pain.

I have met many, many teenagers who believe they are Group 3.

Life has provided a series of perceived misfortunes and now they believe this is just the *way it is*. They have become trapped by their past and don't have the resources or the knowledge to climb out of the emotional 'shock box' they find themselves in.

The most common remedy for this situation in modern culture is medication, leading to the very common misconception that depression is a disease which, in my opinion, and the opinion of many modern psychologists, it is most definitely not. Despite what the media may report, there is very little scientific evidence to suggest that depression is anything other than a damaging emotional pattern.

Let me be very clear, as we discussed in Chapter 4, I'm not saying medication is a bad thing for the right person at the right time, it's just that it's not a cure.

GROUP 3? REALLY? NO, YOU GO FIRST, HONESTLY

Imagine being a modern teenager. Imagine every nasty word, every name someone calls you, every misinterpreted look, every failed test, every party you are not invited to, every embarrassing picture on social media, every person you think is more attractive, more intelligent, more fashionable, more popular or whatever as an electric shock.

And now imagine these shocks happen multiple times a day, every day.

Most of the shocks are administered at school. You have no choice but to expose yourself to them because the people you love the most tell you that you have to go to school. It would be easy to create the perception that the people you love the most are deliberately exposing you to the shocks.

Even though you know that you don't deserve it, the shocks keep coming and there is no lever you can push to make them stop. At least not one you can see.

Other people seem to be able to laugh off their shocks and don't seem bothered at all. How do they do that? Where is the magic 'don't care' switch? Why can't you do that? Could it be it's because you're not as clever as them, not as experienced, not as popular, worth less than them? Yeah that's it isn't it, you're worthless . . .?

Can you see how this pattern of internal criticism forms and delivers shock after shock after shock. Often the issue in people with depressive symptoms is the presence of as many shocks coming from *inside* their own mind as there are from outside.

Friends. *shock*
School. *shock*
Namecalling. *shock*
Party invites. *shock*
Social media. *shock*
Looks. *shock*
Hairstyle. *shock*
Fashion. *shock*

Music. *shock*
Exam results. *shock*
Popularity. *shock*
Worthless. *shock*
Not loved. *shock*

And one I hear often from teenagers,

"Why are the people I love the most putting me through this instead of helping me?"

Shock, anger, shock, pain, shock!

It is inevitable that, given the frequent and persistent 'shocks', teenagers eventually decide that it doesn't matter if they laugh, cry, fight or scream at their life. To them, it appears that nothing is going to change.

They believe they are helpless.

But they are absolutely wrong.

There is every reason to speak up, to fight back, to believe that life can be different.

We are all Group 2 dogs. We have choice. We have the ability to make our escape from discomfort and pain. We are not helpless.

But the story of the Group 3 dogs doesn't end there. There is a mildly positive end to this.

What Seligman and his team did next was to try *teaching* the Group 3 dogs what they needed to do to get away from the shocks. Coaxing them into the safe chamber with treats, rewards or toys did nothing. Neither did physically lifting them from one side to the other. Even after showing the dog that the other chamber was safe and shock free, the next time the experiment ran, the dog would just lie there waiting to be lifted, showing no interest in moving away from the pain.

The dogs had now learned that the only way they would escape the pain was to be lifted and since they couldn't do that themselves, they just endured the pain and waited to be saved.

They still didn't realise that escape was entirely under their own control.

Seligman's team found the only method that worked was for them to physically manipulate each of the dog's legs for them, each step of the way from the 'pain' chamber to the 'safe' one. They had to teach the dogs every single step of the path to escape. The research showed that it took on average, only two experiences of this before the dogs began to associate the physical sensation of their legs moving with escape from pain and make the journey for themselves.

After only *two* experiences, they began to find the resources they needed to change their life for the better.

In the end, these dogs weren't saved; they were helped to save themselves.

Although the methods are distasteful, these experiments illustrate the themes of this book perfectly. The dogs weren't motivated by 'things' (i.e. treats, rewards and toys) and they didn't learn by allowing someone else to save them. They needed lots of support and to be shown how to take responsibility for making changes.

Think of it this way . . . one of our earliest roles as parents is to teach our children how to walk and how to deal with falling down. As they get older we need to teach them to pick themselves up and walk again, and again, and again.

Imagine if you knew that your teen, who currently seems flat, lonely, sad, depressed, angry, down or withdrawn is only two experiences, two rounds of teaching, two short but challenging walks away from coming back to you.

That would totally be worth the effort wouldn't it?

LEARNING TO WALK

Since Seligman's work, the phenomenon of 'learned helplessness' has been studied extensively and it has been found that helplessness has three main types,[9] that I call the 3Ps.

The 3Ps are:

Permanent, Pervasive, Personal.

We can use the 3Ps to help someone back out of the dark place almost as easily as they found their way in.

All we have to do is show the person that each one of the Ps is nothing more than a trick of their mind, each one is, in reality, an illusion.

Illusion #1 – Permanent

As we've seen, it's actually pretty easy to understand how teenagers get themselves stuck in an illusion of permanency, especially with an emotion as significant and powerful as depression. Illusions such as,

---

[9] Peterson, C; Maier, SF; Seligman, MEP. *Learned Helplessness: A Theory for the Age of Personal Control*. New York: Oxford University Press, 1995.

"This is who I am and who I'll always be."

"It's always going to be like this."

"No-one can help me, nothing will ever change."

Statements like these are puddles of permanency.

Remember we discussed that minds, especially teenage ones, 'leak' all over the place and the way to spot the puddle is to listen to what people are saying?

Of course, we can see this is an illusion. It simply isn't true. There is so much time for change, so much still to do, so much still to happen.

But try to imagine what that must be like when the pain doesn't go away like it did before when you were younger. It's new, it's unexpected, it's dark and horrible and you expect it to pass . . . but it doesn't.

Teenagers try and get away from it by immersing themselves in something they enjoy, school work or some other distraction, thinking if they just get on with it for a while, it will all get better just like it has before . . . but it doesn't.

They look to their parents thinking they'll have advice that will make sense of it all. But every time they try to talk to them they don't listen or don't understand or tell them what they did when they were their age.

There's only one conclusion your teenager can draw from all this.

They must be broken and this is the way it is going to be forever.

Without enough experience to know that the power to change every emotional state is within their control, it is inevitable that some teenagers will end up lost in an emotional wilderness, assuming there really is no way out.

But there is.

And I want to show you how to help them find it.

Remember that addressing feelings directly is a short term fix and should be used only in extreme circumstances when you need to 'steady the ship'.

Long term change happens when we change how we think, not how we feel.

To break down the illusion of permanency and influence your teenager's feelings, you need to influence the way they *think*. You can do this with some very simple language techniques that can sneak in under your teen's radar . . . 'stealth parenting' in action!

Read this next statement to yourself and see how it makes you feel (out loud is more effective, unless you're in a public place)!

"I don't know how to get better."

Now add one tiny word and see how things change.

"I don't know how to get better *yet*."

Feels different, doesn't it?

The word 'yet' completely changes the way we perceive a problem because it assumes there *is* a time in the future when you *will* know how to get better. We might not know when that specific time will be but it's definitely coming. It's just not here *yet*.

One little word, three little letters, huge emotional impact.

I am not suggesting that all you have to do is wander into your teen's room, drop a 'yet bomb' at the end of everything they say and walk out having sorted their entire life out.

It doesn't work like that.

This is about breaking the illusion of permanency by continually, consistently and kindly adding *yet* to any suggestion that there is no end, no way out or no solution to the situation your teen is experiencing.

"I don't understand why I feel like this."
"*Yet.*"
"What?"
"You don't understand why you feel like this *yet*. We've only just started talking about it. Let's give it time."

Do you see how that changes the perception of the whole situation?

Using *yet* is just one way to change how we perceive a problem and, to widen your repertoire of linguistic genius, other time-based words like 'soon', 'later', 'now', 'then', etc. will work well too.

"This is who I am and how I feel and that will never change."

"This is who you are and how you feel *now*. Feelings change all the time. This is just how you feel *now*. You didn't feel like this last year and you'll feel different again *soon* but for *now* let's find out why this is happening."

Does that make sense? Can you see what that reply is looking to achieve?

The illusion of permanency can be broken by giving the person the context of time.

Use as many '*yet* bombs', '*now* cannons' and '*soon* bullets' as you possibly can and the illusion will have nowhere to hide! Introducing the concept of time into these statements with the suggestion of a beginning, an end or even both will change the way both you and your teenager think about them.

By using simple language, we can reframe the distorted perception that they have never felt any other way to the way they feel *just now* and show that permanency is an illusion.

Illusion #2 – Pervasive

What if the problem has no end in sight and is also happening all the time, everywhere and just keeps getting worse and worse?

When someone speaks like this you are listening to a big puddle of pervasiveness.

> "It's happening all the time."

> "No-one likes me and no-one cares."

> "Everyone hates me."

Each of these 'leaked' phrases contains a clue that the mind is seeing this problem everywhere and all the time. No breaks, no gaps, no respite.

If it isn't already everywhere in their life, then it soon will be.

Before we look at this illusion in more detail, let's just clarify once again . . .

**a negative emotional state is proof
that the mind is working perfectly.**

As the mind begins to believe any new pattern of thought is real, for example "I am not good enough", it starts to apply that pattern to everything it sees.

If that belief is strong enough confirmation bias will take over. This means our mind will remember anything that confirms our beliefs and discard anything that doesn't. Slowly but surely the problem will show up all over the place and only because we believe it to be real.

Imagine you are 14 and dye your hair green and pierce your lip. Someone in a corridor at school calls you 'wierdo' and it makes you feel vulnerable, scared, alone. It is a 'shock', just like the dogs from earlier.

That thought rattles around your head, replaying again and again and then it begins to spread. You begin to wonder if anyone else thinks the same thing.

Every little sideways look that someone gives you now hides a judgmental smile.

Because you are weird.

Every giggle in the corridor and whisper in the classroom is, in your mind, now aimed at you.

Because you are weird.

Every time someone talks to you, you prepare to defend yourself.

Because you are weird.

It doesn't matter if the sideways look didn't actually exist, the whisper was about someone else or if the worst doesn't happen, your mind has convinced itself you are weird and you are now trapped in the Illusion of Pervasiveness.

To break this illusion you have to first remember that it might have some basis in truth.

If you are 14, dye your hair green and pierce your lip then people *are* going to look and stare. That is what happens to anyone perceived not to fit with what the majority consider to be 'normal'. But that doesn't mean it's happening *everywhere* and it also doesn't mean you're weird.

And there's the first clue to the language techniques we can use to help.

Words like 'all', 'every', 'no-one', 'everyone', 'always' and 'never' imply that there is nothing else apart from what is happening right now.

"I'm *never* going understand this."

"I *always* get *everything* wrong."

"I'm *totally* useless and *no-one* likes me."

I'm going to let you in on one of the simplest linguistic techniques there is to break this illusion. All you have to do is listen for the 'trigger' word and say it back with a question mark on the end.

For example;

"I'm never going to understand this"
"*Never*?"

"I always get everything wrong"
"*Always*?" and/or "*Everything*?"

"I'm totally useless and no-one likes me"
"*Totally*?" and/or "*No-one*?"

Responses to this type of questioning are predictable and often comical!

"Well, of course I know I don't *always* get *everything* wrong, but . . . oh, just shut up, you know what I mean!"

Again, we are challenging thoughts rather than feelings. If we get someone to realise that it isn't *always*, or *never*, or *no-one* then we will change the way they think forever.

Forever?

Yes! Forever.

If someone believes no-one loves them and you show them that just one person loves them dearly, you have started a process of change. The thought that *no-one* loves them can *never* be true again.

Never?

Never. The illusion of pervasiveness has been broken.

You will need to break it again should the feelings crop up in the future, but you just keep breaking it until it can never repair itself.

Never?

OK, I'll stop that now, I think you get the point!

But remember . . . *you* must not stop. Once you've helped put one foot forward, you must keep going until they are walking unaided.

The shocks will keep coming, and each time they do you must challenge their illusions, teach them how to respond and help them stand up and escape the pain all by themselves.

We don't want our teens to become Group 3 dogs – so numb that they feel the shocks and just don't care. We want them to accept there are places, people and situations that are safe, that do offer escape and that in those places they are free to express and enjoy and be themselves.

Illusion #3 – Personal

It is really important to help our teenagers understand that, special as they are, the universe does not actually revolve around them.

This is the third and last of our Ps – *Personal*. I call this one the 'all about me' illusion.

"No-one understands *me*."

"Why do these things *always* happen to *me*?"

"I*'m* so pathetic and useless and this is just more proof."

It is very common for people, especially teenagers, to think that their problems are significantly bigger than everyone else's.

Teenage problems, even those caused because Craig has fallen out with Connor, or Richard has broken up with Lisa (no matter how upset she might be), are only important to a very small group of people. To pretty much everyone else on the planet, they are entirely insignificant.

Being surrounded by the drama and emotion of growing up means that problems are not very hard to find for teenagers. There will always be a fall out, a break up, an argument, a cross word, nasty name or bitchy comment because that's what happens when you and everyone around you, is practicing the skills of being an adult.

Think back to the Group 3 dogs. That type of experience is a lonely one, accepting there is nothing you can do and no-one is coming to help. It makes sense to give up, lie down and accept the pain. Because you aren't anything like the other dogs, it's easier to separate yourself and become disconnected from the group.

Our teens do this too.

Breaking this illusion starts with teaching your teen to realise that they are loved, cared for, appreciated and that someone is there to listen to them. This, as we have discussed, is not always as easy as we would like it to be.

Remember the Two Teen Questions? Those questions mean that being loved and appreciated by our parents is often taken for granted – you are their 'normal', the baseline of their life. Your love is unquestioned. In their mind, your love has always been there and always will be and that's why they are more than likely completely ignoring that it even exists!

To break the 'all about me' illusion, you need to remind them, in a way that they can no longer ignore, that they are loved, you are there for them and you're not going to leave them alone with their pain.

To do this, you don't have to become their best friend, drink fruity cider at parties and hang with your homies at the park, man.

No. That would be tragic.

All you need to do is climb into their false reality . . . and smash it to pieces!

This isn't as difficult or as dramatic as it sounds.

You already know how to see the world through their eyes. If you accept and understand *any* and *all* of their emotional states, I promise your teen will begin to feel love, trust and begin to open up to you.

This does not mean I am advising you to get in any way involved in the stuff between Craig and Connor, or Richard and Lisa, or any of their other many teenage dramas.

All you need to do is learn to ask good questions.

Here's a couple of crackers to get the illusion-busting process rolling.

'And that means . . .?'

and

'Because . . .?'

A bit like Ant and Dec, there's really no point in having just one of these without the other. Together they work to keep a conversation going while you find out what is *really* going on.

Don't jump to conclusions, don't offer answers or help (yet), don't ask them why or try and force them to do what you think they should do (it's not about you remember!), at this stage you are only finding out the internal mechanism of how this person's thoughts work.

As a very general guide, 'And that means . . .?' is for actions and triggers and 'Because . . .?' is for feelings.

Here's an example of how a conversation might go.

"I missed the bus this morning, came in late and Mr Blackmore shouted at me in front of the whole class."

   "OK, *and that means . . .?*"

"It means I can never go back to school."

"*Because . . .?*"

"Because he totally humiliated me and I feel so embarrassed."

"*Because . . .?*"

"What do you mean, because?"

"*You are humiliated because . . .?*"

"Because everyone was there and saw him shouting at me."

"*And that means . . .?*"

"They will all be talking about me."

"*And that means . . .?*"

"They'll all think I'm an idiot?"

Do you see how this works?

With just a few questions you have discovered that the real problem isn't being shouted at, it's a hidden fear that everyone thinks they are an idiot.

Your role is to gently nudge things forwards and keep the conversation going until you get to the root of the problem. As you become an expert in using this type of language (which will only happen through practice), you can mix in all the other challenges such as '*never?*' and '*everyone?*' to really drill down through the smokescreen until the opportunity for you use their own reality to break the illusion is presented.

In our example above 'They'll all think I'm stupid' is the illusion that needs to be broken and we break it with one simple request – we ask for evidence.

What proof, evidence or facts can your teen provide to back up this statement?

Has someone said something? Have they seen something about themselves on social media, heard a rumour, been told by someone? If they do have concrete evidence, and even though the personal nature of the issue is still an illusion (not *everyone* thinks your teen is an idiot), the causes for it are real and you *must* deal with it in an appropriate way. They are looking for you to be a Role Model here. If, for example, you find your teen is being bullied on social media then this is not the time to break illusions, it's the time to show them you have their back and address the issue.[10]

Happily, in most cases, they can provide no evidence. They might try! They may even try and make some up but that is easy to challenge. Keep it as light and as inquisitive as possible. Don't think of this as an attack on their reality, think of it more like a puzzle. You are looking to find the chink in the armour, the gap in the defence, the weak link in the chain.

Once you find it, there is no choice but to see that the personal nature of their problems is just another illusion.

Approach all of these conversations with acceptance and understanding, see the world through their eyes, point out any and every break in the evidence and you will shrink the problem down to a more manageable size.

Words have power and you have some very powerful words that will begin a process of change for you and your family.

OUT OF MY BOX

The skills you are learning here help you become a modern parent. A parent who is there for their teenager as they deal with a world

---

[10] Please remember to listen and stay calm. This is not the time for you to lose your cool and forget about acceptance and understanding. Screaming about how bad the school is or why it has taken so long for you to hear about this is not going to help. The only thing you have to do is work out the best and quickest way to deal with the situation and your teenager may be able to help with that.

you, and they, don't fully understand. A world that never switches off.

It is easy for teenagers to become anxious, stressed or stuck in a cycle of helplessness because there is nowhere to escape from the pressure created by technology and social media.

Of course, we all have a choice. We could avoid social media altogether. But, as a teenager, how would you fit in if you weren't where everyone else was?

As a parent, you need to be strong. You are their certainty, even when they treat you badly. They need to know they can rely on you, that they can lean on you and that you will be there for them no matter what.

It is vital that you have the skills to help your teen cope with the emotions that result from their early entry into this adult world. Our teenagers are being asked to develop a diverse emotional range at a much earlier age than we ever were. Children as young as eight are being diagnosed with anxiety, depression and other emotional issues and it is my belief that these conditions do not need to be medicated as long as the people closest to them know how to spot the signs and know how to help.

Your teenager is leaking all over your house.

Look for the puddles.

Chapter 6 – What The . . . ?

- The modern world is putting extraordinary pressure on our children. They live in a world with no escape from the pressures of school, growing up and the emotional drama of being a teenager.

- We can class most teenage issues as the result of one of three emotional states; anxiety ('what if . . . ?), stress (over-whelm) and depression (helplessness).

- Stress is the result of too much stuff squeezing into too little space. Help your teen empty their mind and do it regularly!

- Helplessness is the result of three perceived illusions – permanency (always/never), pervasiveness (everywhere) and personal (all about me).

- These illusions can be shattered forever by simply using the right questions at the right time. Forever? Yes, forever!

7

Being Good People

What do you think is the single, most important quality in a person? I'm asking you about the most vital, important characteristic that you think every other human should display.

If I was to ask you to expand that one vital quality to the three most important qualities in a person, what would your list look like?

I'm going to make a prediction that your answers included attributes such as kindness, humour, warmth, confidence, generosity, compassion, happiness, gratitude, drive, helping others, ambition, resilience, confidence, empathy and other positive emotions that bring good things to the world. I'm also going to guess that you did not include academic qualifications, sensible career choices, above average intellectual ability or the size of their social circle.

Let me give you a scenario to consider.

You are interviewing for a new position in your company and you have whittled it down to two candidates.

Candidate 1 received an exceptional education at one of the best schools in the country. However, during the interview process, they have been mildly rude to all interviewers and their answers have been very short. All the interviewers noted that the candidate talked about themselves *a lot* and they are fiercely competitive and ambitious. They are perfectly qualified for the role and have ample experience.

Candidate 2 had a good education at an average school where they got an average set of results. The interview team all commented on how polite and warm the candidate has been to everyone they met and how every question has been rewarded with interesting, full answers. They have a proven track record of teamwork and have great results from their previous job. They are ambitious yet have an honest attitude to their ability. They have absolutely no experience in the role you are interviewing for and don't have the degree level education requested as part of the application.

Which one do you want to hire?

I would imagine the majority of us would lean towards hiring Candidate 2 because we are naturally drawn to people who like people. Our lives are defined by the quality of our relationships and, to be quite frank, I don't think Candidate 1 is someone who would foster good quality working relationships!

I said to you right at the beginning of this book that there was just one certainty of parenthood.

Something you do is going to totally mess your kid up.

But there is one safeguard you can put in place to ensure any parental mess up is nothing more than a mild inconvenience.

Help them be a good person.

As parents we can all too easily become obsessed with the pursuit of our teenager's success, too focused on protecting them from the perils of the future, too wrapped up in the mantra of 'not making the same mistakes I made', and too forgetful that we, their parents, are moving through life despite all our mistakes and we have ended up, pretty much, OK.

If I could teach parents just one thing, it would be to focus on the *person* your teenager is becoming before you focus on exam results and the subjective successes of their teenage years.

A list of A grades on a certificate and successes in sport, academia or some other pursuit is, of course, amazing. We all want these proud moments with our kids, but they aren't everything.

Once school days are over, and they will be soon, it's their qualities as a person that will define the quality of their life.

As you think about your teenager can you honestly say they are a good person? Are they warm, kind, loving and all those other things you said above that you wanted to see in a person, even if you need to look for that warmth and kindness under a cloud of stress, anxiety or helplessness?

If you can then you have done your job and you have done it well.

And that, right there, is the whole point of parenting.

We don't know what the future will bring. We know what it looks like now and we know what's happened in the past, but we can only ever guess at what is going to happen next.

As parents we forget that, especially as we have progressed in our career, much of our progress and success in life has less to do with academic achievements and much more to do with being a good person who demonstrates a good, robust set of values.

I am not saying that you should tell your kids to stop studying and forget university or whatever they want to do next, far from it. What I'm asking is for you to listen, let your teenager be themselves while you do your very best to make sure they are good people who have everything they need to be a success.

Some parents have very academic children, some have artistic children, some have children who can weave and craft a story, some have children who can do amazing things with their hands, some have dyslexic children or autistic children, or children that defy any category.

All these 'types' of children will have very different aspirations and aims but all of them can be good people.

All teenagers benefit from a mentor (that can be you!) to help them become an asset to the world in whatever way that may be. While you might have picked up this book to help you work out how you can stop your future entrepreneur or bestselling author from dying their hair green, I hope you now understand that your teenager has every chance of becoming someone really special whatever their hair colour.

Dying their hair green isn't really as important as the qualities that they show as a person.

Your job is to nurture and support those qualities.

As we close this book, it's really important to understand the pitfalls of chasing the wrong types of success for your teenager. But, on the off chance you do make this mistake, or any of the others we have discussed I have a solution. I am going to teach you . . .

the six most powerful words in the universe.

All I ask is you remember these six little words when everything is going wrong and repeat them quietly to yourself as the bedroom door slams and another family dance ends with a huffy teenager retreating to their room claiming no-one loves them.

The Six Most Powerful Words in The Universe are very easy to remember . . .

everything is going to be OK.

I promise.

I know there are things that can't be easily undone – bad tattoos, stretched ear lobes, physical scars and the like – but that doesn't mean that someone's life is over or ruined. It just means they made a decision that may, or may not, turn out to be a good one.

And if it's not a good one, that's your cue to recite, quietly and confidently inside your head,

everything is going to be OK.

It may not seem like it now but it will be.

Have patience, keep focused on where you're going rather than where you are, stay strong, and everything *will* be OK.

Life is a long game, the longest game you'll ever play, yet we act as if it can all be catastrophically ruined in these six short teenage years. Although this is true in some very extreme cases, for the vast majority, and you're very likely to be in the vast majority, it's not true at all.

In fact, for the vast majority, even when all seems lost,

everything is going to be OK.

You are a key player in making sure your kids are going to be OK. You have influence but you have to use that influence wisely.

Remember you are dealing with an adult in training, not a child and,

everything is going to be OK.

Your teen is getting ready to leave your pride. They are about to take that long walk off into the jungle of life. Your job, from the day they were born, has been to make sure they are ready when that day comes.

Praise, celebrate and reminisce on their success.

Support, help and guide when it all goes wrong.

Be a critic but don't criticise. Offer acceptance and understanding in every instance.

It is vital you have an opinion but remember it is *how* that opinion is delivered that is the key to achieving long term success and change.

Help your teenager apply good labels. Their belief in themselves will define much of what happens over the coming years.

Listen and notice how they are making the decisions they need to make. Dilemma is inevitable; be a good model, show them the way by acting on what you say.

B*e* the person you want *them* to be.

Walk your talk.

Your teenager will be stressed, anxious or even feel helpless at times, but if you reflect that back to them you will simply become part of the problem. They want to be safe and to be loved. We all want that. E*specially* at those times when all seems lost and the proverbial has hit the fan.

Take time to learn their code and figure out what motivates them. You don't have to work hard on this, they will be leaking their code, along with every other emotion, all over your house!

But remember, fear is a powerful motivator and will hide in even the most confident of teenagers.

It's up to you to spot the puddles.

Use your 'whys' carefully, a life's mission is hard to find but even a small hint at what that could be will be a far more powerful motivator than a new jacket or phone.

And remember *no-one* is ever broken. Including you.

Your parenting mistakes are just part of you learning to be a grown up.

Your teenager's mistakes are the same.

I know that if you take the pressure off yourself and stop trying to be perfect, your journey of learning will ultimately bring you happiness and parenting success.

I hope this book has helped you decode your teenager and maybe even decode a little bit of yourself.

Go back to your family and . . .

make good people.

Chapter 7 – What The . . . ?

- There is nothing more important than teaching your child to be a good person.

- To make a good person, *be* a good person.

- Good people will find success, no matter what their teenage achievements or disasters.

- Just relax, you've got this.

- Everything is going to be OK.

Epilogue:
Being Number One

Before I go, I want to take a brief opportunity to talk about someone important that we have neglected over the course of this book.

You.

There is something that happens in many families and, although it causes huge difficulties, it is often entirely hidden from everyone involved. It also has absolutely nothing to do with your teenager.

Let me show you . . .

Assuming all the following decisions were happening at the same time, rank them in order of importance *to you*.

1. Your partner asks you to go out for dinner, just the two of you.
2. The kids have clubs/parties/things.
3. You want to go to a one-off evening class to learning something you are really interested in.

What would be your personal order of importance? Who would 'win'? Come on . . . be honest.

In my experience, the most common answer is 2 (the kids) would come first and definitely make their clubs even if it means rearranging the whole evening around this, 3 (the class) would be next on the list and would happen if you could arrange it around the kids and then finally, 1 (dinner) would likely never happen because you're just too busy with everything else.

Next most common is 2 (kids), 1(dinner), 3(class). The kids get first shout, the course is ditched and dinner happens but again, only if it can be squeezed in around the kids and it's nothing fancy, just a quick bite at the local Indian buffet still dressed in your work clothes.

The issue here is not classes, or dinner, or clubs. The issue is how you prioritise your life.

If you are regularly putting the kids first, above ALL else, I promise it will be causing hidden problems.

I'll tell you right now, the order that creates what I call the Perfect Family Dynamic, is;

You first,

your partner/relationship second,

and the kids third.

You're shifting uncomfortably in your seat, aren't you? Most people do when I tell them this!

Here's a wee test . . . when you come in from work at night, if your partner and kids are in the house when you arrive home, who gets your attention first?

Let me guess based on the most common answer again, 2, 3, 1 – Kids, you, your partner.

If your partner was to suggest a romantic date night with dinner and the cinema, they have to fight past the kids' needs and your needs before they get to spend quality time with you.

If this is true for you, I want you to realise your partner is often third best. And, unconsciously, they know it.

If your work is an important part of your life, they may even slip to fourth behind that report that just needs to be done for Monday.

Over a short period of time this isn't a problem. Sometimes it just needs to be this way. When our kids are babies, we all know they demand and need a lot of your time and attention. It is a fact of life that our priorities must change during this time. Many relationships don't survive this stage for that very reason. One part of the couple can't cope with being 'down the pecking order'.

But once they are teenagers? After 14 years of being third choice, your partner will be feeling it and they will know there is no reason for it still to be this way.

In fact, I wouldn't be surprised to find, if it has been going on long enough, they may have just stopped asking for your time and attention.

It would not surprise me if being third best in each other's lives has become one of you and your partner's most well rehearsed, and most often ignored, family dances.

By the way, in my experience moving your partner up to second best, meaning you prioritise them over yourself (but still not quite as much as the kids) doesn't change anything.

They will still know the kids beat them in the decision making stakes every single time. There is still no point in asking for a date night because little Sarah's dancing lessons are always more important.

Over time, you train your partner to know where they are in your priorities. There becomes no reason to ask for your time or your attention. They know the answer before they ask the question.

"But, of course my kids are number one! They have to be."

I hear this all the time and I will admit it seems very sensible that your mission to be a good parent puts your kids at number one. But I've got to tell you . . . you've got it wrong!

They ask and things happen. They need to be taken somewhere, they need money, clothes, help with homework, whatever and they get it. They see their parent(s) sacrifice themselves for their demands time after time and, over time, it becomes normal.

They ask, you deliver.

They are more important than you and they are more important than your relationship.

Every time.

It's important to realise that they are not taking advantage of this on purpose. It is all they know. This is their experience. This is what you taught them life is like and, as you have learned, they will continue in any pattern you have taught them.

At least until you teach them a new pattern.

Life isn't always going to be like this. They won't always be number one and when they're not, what life experience will they have to help them through?

And as for you?

If the kids are first in every decision, you are placing yourself second or third best in your own life! You've become a victim of your own love and support. Being second or third best, means losing your passions, abandoning your personal missions, shelving your personal goals and ambitions. Your moments of glory are often not yours, they are your children's moments of glory that you get to revel in and be part of . . . at least for now.

Your kids are growing every year and now, especially as teenagers, they are coming close to leaving your family home and going off to live their own life. What will you do then?

Do you remember how to have a mission that isn't focused on your children?

Do you remember who you are?

When your children leave and that part of your life evolves, will you and your partner have a relationship left? Will it go back to where you left off all those years ago or will you both realise how much you have changed? Will your values still match? Will the things you enjoyed sharing and doing together when you were young, carefree and childfree have changed?

If this all sounds harsh, I apologise but it's meant to be! I want to shock you into making a change that will benefit your life, improve your relationship and safeguard your children and your family for the future.

As a reminder, over my years of experience and in my own life, the most successful, happy, loving, nurturing and perfect family dynamic is you first, your partner next, then the kids.

Let me be really clear about what I'm saying here.

You have to be number one in your life.

When you put yourself first *everyone* benefits. And, for balance, the same advice is true for your partner. When they put themselves first, *everyone* benefits.

I was going to design a clever metaphor to explain this but there's no need because one already exists!

When you sit on a plane and they tell you how to behave in an emergency situation they give you a really important survival tip – place your own oxygen mask on before helping others with theirs.

This isn't just an emergency survival tip, it's excellent advice for life.

By putting yourself at number one, you begin living a life where all, or at least many, of your passions, missions and goals are being fulfilled. You go to that class, you go for that job, you look after your needs and do the things that inspire, motivate and energise *you*.

People say to me all the time, "But Brian, that's selfish!" I explain that all I'm really asking is for them to start thinking about their own needs and looking after themselves. How can that possibly be selfish?

I promise that when you begin fulfilling your passions and making decisions that benefit you on an entirely personal level, you will have more energy, you will be happier and you will be a nicer, more positive person to be around.

I want you to make decisions as yourself, not as Molly's dad or Jamie's mum.

I am asking you to reclaim your identity. To remember who you are.

When you do that you will find being a parent is now a huge part of your identity, it's just not everything. That means spending time with the family is still something that you look forward to, something that nourishes your soul and that means *everyone* wins.

You will still do the run to the clubs but you are doing it because you want to, not because you have to.

Being a parent is only a very small part of being you. There is so much more to you than just being a mum or a dad. It's time to remember that and embrace it.

When you get it right, it becomes a perfect balance of passion, responsibility and necessity.

Think of some of the truly happy people you know, people who beam positivity. They never make themselves victims. They are people who do what they need to do to be the best they can be and have engineered their lives to have balance.

And that balance, that perfect family dynamic, will also reflect into your relationship where one of two things typically happens.

Sometimes, having decided to put yourself first, you look at your relationship and see that it isn't how you want it to be or what you thought it was and maybe it hasn't been for a while.

Putting yourself first, you realise that 'staying together for the kids' or 'just putting up with it for a bit longer' isn't working any more so you start a mission to change it. The motivation will be easy to find because you will refuse to leave it like it is. You, your partner and your kids are too important to let it stay this way.

If this is happening in your life (and if it isn't), remember that, from a very young age, your kids are watching you. You are their model. You are teaching them about relationships right now. Your relationship is their most detailed model of what a loving couple look like and they will base their future relationships on what they see.

Would you want a relationship like yours for your son or daughter?

Have the tough conversations, be honest about how you feel, listen to your partner and look for *their* patterns and motivations. Get back on the same page. Do everything you can to make it work and if that is just not possible then you do what is right and you get out.

A client I had a few years ago, told me something I have never forgotten and I pass it to you now in the hope it may make sense to you if you are in this situation. He said "Looking back to my childhood, I now realise it's better to come from a broken home than to live in one".

Happily, the far more common scenario when you decide to put yourself first, is that your partner jumps on board and does the same, and we get two happy, fulfilled people in a relationship which only becomes stronger and stronger.

You and your partner understand that both of you have an important life away from the kids and that, as a couple, you are both vital to the family. If you are happy, both individually and together, how can the whole family be anything but happy?

Being together and making good choices about each other's needs and remembering the small things – the goodbye kiss, the coming home cuddle or even just asking "How was your day?" – these all go a long way towards making everyone feel loved, secure and happy.

In a perfect dynamic there are two adults who are happy, fulfilled and living a life that fulfils both their emotional codes. They each have their own individual identities that come together to make a rock solid couple. This means, as a partnership, they are loving, close and warm. They support each other when they make mistakes, they know they can't be perfect. They simply do all they can to be good people.

Can you imagine this couple having sad children?

Whether they are young kids or teenagers, the children in this family are learning from ideal models who are showing them through their actions, words and values how to be happy and fulfilled both on a personal level *and* in a relationship.

In this family, *everyone* feels loved and secure.

The children in this family know they are never alone while also learning that the world does *not* revolve around them. They hear the word 'no' and they hear it because their parents have decided that, this time, the grown ups will decide what's going to happen.

They respect it, because they understand balance. They don't know why they understand it but they do! It just feels as if it's the way it's meant to be.

Everyone is happy. *Everyone* feels loved. *Everyone* is secure.

I hope as you read this little epilogue you realised that you already live in the perfect family dynamic. OK, it might not be 'perfect', I don't really think perfect is possible, but what you have is good, healthy and positive.

I wish you continued happiness and fulfilment for the future.

If you are recognising something else then I have a challenge for you.

For the next ten days, I want you to put yourself first. I want you to think about yourself as number one, I want you to break the dances you have established and I want you to be happy.

Ten days. Can you gift yourself just 10 days to be happy?

How do you do that . . .?

This whole book has taught you how.

Right here, at the end of the book, I'm going to let you into a secret.

This book isn't really about teenagers. It's about *people*.

If you didn't notice, I urge you to reflect on all you have read and appreciate just how much you have learned about yourself as you have read these pages.

It's important to understand that *we are all the same*.

We, the parents of this world, are teenagers that have grown up (a bit).

We have dilemmas, anxieties and moments where we don't know what to do.

We look for models to help us grow and learn that there aren't as many of them around as there were when we were young.

Inside, we still have moments where we feel like a teenager, want to dye our hair green and get a new tattoo.

It's just that our values and priorities have changed as we've got older and so we are not as impulsive anymore. We worry about maintaining an identity that fits what we think society expects from us.

But that doesn't mean we don't *want to*!

Sometimes, it's nice to go crazy at a gig or drink too much and stay out until 6am. It just hurts a lot more than it used to and, since pain is such an effective motivator, we do it far less often than when we were 19!

Stay young inside and put yourself, and your relationship, at the top of your pile.

Remember, our goal as parents isn't to be perfect. It's to make good people.

And those good people must include *you*.

Dear Parents,

Your book has now finished, thanks very much for reading. I hope you've enjoyed it, learned loads and I'm really looking forward to getting your feedback and reviews. If you pop your comments on Amazon via this link rcbks.com/teenamazon I'll see them and you'll feel good about the fact that you will be helping other parents just like you discover this book and benefit from the same cool stuff you've just learned.

But don't go just yet!

You'll notice there are a few pages left.

They're not for you.

I'd like you to gently suggest to your teenager that they have a look at these pages. Don't freak them out by asking them to read the whole book, just these four pages and that's all . . . for now.

Let's see what happens after that shall we?

Thank you for taking the time to read my book. I really do appreciate you allowing me to help.

B.

An Ending
Introduction

Hi.

You have no clue who I am and, pretty obviously, I've absolutely no clue who you are either. But I'm wide[1] enough to think I can help you without us having ever said hello in person.

I help people of all ages make their lives easier. I help find calm when everything is going a bit mental. I help find confidence and certainty when people doubt themselves. I help people understand why other people make them want to scream.

I don't order people about, I don't tell them what to do and I definitely don't tell them what *not* to do. My personal view is if you particularly want a tattoo then go right ahead (I'd still recommend you avoid your face though!)

You might want to get pierced as many times as will make you happy.

You might want to get drunk (for legal reasons, let me be clear that I mean only when you are legally permitted to drink, of course).

You might want to go to parties and get with people you wish you hadn't.

Of course, you don't *have* to do any of these things if you don't want to. But if you do, I'm not going to stop you and I won't ever tell you it's wrong.

But before you do any of those things can you please do me one huge favour?

I really want you to understand why your parents can sometimes be such king size pains in the arse.

---

[1] For our non-Scottish readers, wide = cheeky.

I want you to understand why they moan, why your curfew is so early, why they shout when you make stupid, wee mistakes that don't matter and why they won't get off your back about life in general.

And so that you can understand, I need to let you into a secret that's just between us.

They have been reading this book thinking it's all about you. It's called Cracking The Teen Code and, if you are reading these few pages, I guarantee they will be well chuffed with themselves that they read this book right to the end and learned some new parenting stuff.

They will speak to their pals about the serious parenting points they have earned by reading a book about the psychology of teenagers.

But the book wasn't just about teenagers.

It was about them too.

Be prepared for them to start coming at you with all sorts of new questions and acting really weird. It might be a pain at first but I promise it's all good. I told them to do that and they really are trying to do things better than they did before. Or, at the very least, if they can't manage to do things better then they should be doing them differently.

Everything I have taught them is to help them and you have a happier life. Give them a break as they try these new things on and they are really, really trying to be the best parent(s) they can be.

I'm Brian, I'm an expert in the mind and emotions. I work with teenagers all the time and I know lots about why your mind does the things it does. I go into schools and talk to young people, like you, about how to make the pressures of growing up a little easier to handle and how to make good decisions about life in general.

I don't believe that you need success in school and amazing exam results to have a happy life and I want you to know that I haven't cooked up some trick with your parents to get you studying more.

I just want to help you make sense of the crazy emotional stuff that seems to keep happening around you and make living with your folks just that little bit easier.

So can I ask you my favour now?

I want *you* to read this book.

It's not very long and you don't have to read it all at once. Just try a wee bit at a time and see if you can recognise yourself.

I think you'll be surprised!

I'd recommend you skip the whole of Chapter 1. We talk about stuff in that chapter that you haven't experienced yet (like having babies!) so you'll probably be bored stiff by that bit.

Start with chapter 2 and realise that, even though it often mentions 'teens' and 'your teenager', the whole book is really about *people*. And, they might not act like it sometimes but your parents are also people – this book is about them as much as you.

I want you to understand why they do what they do and, as a wee bonus, you will also learn why you do what you do at the same time.

I promise there's lots of interesting stuff in here, I tell lots of stories about people you probably know, it's not super serious and I have at least tried to make it as funny as I can. I even call Buzz Lightyear an arsehole at one point and if that doesn't get you at least flicking through to find out why then my wee plea has fallen on deaf ears!

Now the choice is yours.

You can put the book down and leave it or you can let me show you why I say Buzz Lightyear is an arsehole and, even though you might think it sometimes, why your parents (and you) are not.

I hope you make a good choice but whatever you choose, remember when you were born you didn't come with an instruction manual and we're all making it up as we go along. That means your parents have more than likely made some mistakes. And so have you.

Wouldn't life be a whole lot easier if we had some sort of instruction manual?

Of course it would!

I hope you take a little bit of time to read the rest of this book and find out how all of this life stuff works.

Whatever you decide, take care of yourself and do good things.

Brian